Reading STREET

Grade 3

Scott Foresman

Fresh Reads

for Fluency and Comprehension

PEARSON

Glenview, Illinois • Boston, Massachusetts • Chandler, Arizona • Upper Saddle River, New Jersey

ISBN 13: 978-0-328-48895-7
ISBN 10: 0-328-48895-X
9 10 V0N4 18 17 16 15 14 13 12

PEARSON

Contents

Unit 1 Living and Learning

Unit 2 Smart Solutions

Unit 3 People and Nature

Unit 4 One of a Kind

Unit 5 Cultures

Unit 6 Freedom

Name ______________________________

Read the selection. Then answer the questions that follow.

Lucky Lucy

Lucy Mouse was excited. Today a new mouse was coming to class.

"Meet our new student, Ted Mouse," said Mr. Toad. "Let's make him feel welcome."

No one said a word. They were all staring because Ted had no tail!

At lunch, no one invited Ted to join them. Lucy felt sorry for Ted, but she was going to sit with her friends. Then she slipped and dropped all her food. No one said a word. They all just stared at her.

Only Ted walked over to Lucy. He said, "Don't worry. I'll help you."

Ted helped Lucy get more food. Then Ted and Lucy ate lunch together.

Turn the page.

Answer the questions below.

1 **Which of these showed that Ted Mouse was kind?**

- ◯ He helped Lucy.
- ◯ He came to class.
- ◯ He ate his lunch.
- ◯ He was a new student.

2 **What happened at the *end* of the story?**

- ◯ Mr. Toad introduced Ted Mouse.
- ◯ Ted Mouse ate lunch with Lucy Mouse.
- ◯ Lucy Mouse dropped her food.
- ◯ The students stared at Ted Mouse.

3 **Where did this story take place?**

- ◯ on the playground
- ◯ in the library
- ◯ on the bus
- ◯ in school

4 **What lesson did Lucy learn in this story?**

Name ______________________________________

Read the selection. Then answer the questions that follow.

Sanya's Science Report

Sanya was tired of looking at her screen and turned to look out the window. It was raining on Planet Octor. Sanya had to write a report for science class about a planet she had never visited.

Sanya's mom came into the room. "Why aren't you reading your teaching screen?" she asked.

"Oh, I have been. I've decided to write about Earth," Sanya said. "Why don't we go there? I can't think of a better way to learn about a planet."

Mom agreed, so they jumped into their spaceship and headed for Earth. Sanya looked out the window as they traveled. She recognized Norbeed, a red planet she and her family had visited on vacation. It still had a red halo around it.

Sanya knew from her teaching screen that Earth was different from Octor and Norbeed. Earth was a planet of blue water and green land. After three days, the blue and green planet came into view. Just as the spaceship was coming into landing orbit, Sanya heard a loud noise.

"Don't worry," Mom said. "That's just a signal from the Earth crew letting us know they're ready to pull us in."

Sanya smiled. She was eager to learn about Planet Earth.

Turn the page.

Answer the questions below.

1 **What was the *most important* event in the story?**

- ◯ Sanya's mom came into the room.
- ◯ Sanya and her mom flew to Earth.
- ◯ Sanya heard a loud noise from Earth.
- ◯ Sanya's spaceship passed Norbeed.

2 **Where was Sanya at the *beginning* of the story?**

- ◯ on a long trip
- ◯ in a spaceship
- ◯ at school
- ◯ at home

3 **What happened at the *end* of the story?**

- ◯ Sanya recognized the color of Norbeed.
- ◯ Sanya and her mother visited Earth.
- ◯ Sanya decided to write about Planet Earth.
- ◯ Sanya and her mother went on vacation.

4 **Which word *best* describes Sanya?**

- ◯ curious
- ◯ afraid
- ◯ lonely
- ◯ sleepy

5 **What did this story teach you about how to learn about something new?**

____

____

____

____

____

____

____

____

Name ______________________________

Read the selection. Then answer the questions that follow.

The Fire Stealer

Once upon a time, there was no fire on the Earth, and animals everywhere were freezing. They could see the fire in the sun but could not get even a tiny coal from fierce Firekeeper, the sun's guardian. One day the animals were so cold they decided to take some fire.

Brave Crow said, "I will fly to the sun and take a piece of coal. Firekeeper will not miss such a tiny piece."

But Firekeeper noticed him and was so furious that he burned the feathers off of Crow's head as punishment.

Then Wily Possum said, "Maybe I can take some fire and hide it in my tail. Firekeeper will not notice a small coal hidden in my bushy tail."

But Possum could not fool Firekeeper, and angry Firekeeper burned the fur off Possum's tail as punishment.

Finally, tiny Water Spider said, "I will get so wet that the sun cannot burn me, and I will spin thread to make a little bowl on my back where I can carry the small piece of fire that I take."

Water Spider was so small she could easily slip by Firekeeper. When the animals saw her carrying back the fire, they all cheered.

Bear said, "You are the smallest in our animal family, yet you gave us this precious gift of fire."

Turn the page.

Answer the questions below.

1 **Based on Water Spider's actions, you can say that she was**

- ◯ small and afraid.
- ◯ smart and brave.
- ◯ big and strong.
- ◯ sad and lonely.

2 **This story took place at a time when**

- ◯ the sun was not hot.
- ◯ animals lost their fire.
- ◯ the Earth was a cold place.
- ◯ animals lived in coal mines.

3 **How was Water Spider like a real person?**

- ◯ The sun could not burn her.
- ◯ She was so small she could hardly be seen.
- ◯ She went to visit Firekeeper.
- ◯ She made a plan to do something.

4 **What happened at the *end* of the story?**

____

____

____

____

____

5 **What lesson did the characters learn in this story?**

____

____

____

____

____

____

Name ______________________________

Read the selection. Then answer the questions that follow.

First Place

Gene woke up nervous. The music contest was on Monday. Gene was scared.

"I can't do it," Gene said to his parents.

"First you need to practice. I will help you," Gene's dad said. They practiced the piano together every day.

Then Gene and his dad went to the contest. Gene heard the other students play. They played very well. *I don't have a chance*, Gene thought to himself.

Later it was Gene's turn. He looked at his dad and felt better. Gene played without any mistakes. He could not believe it when he heard his name called as the first-place winner.

Finally, Gene wasn't nervous anymore.

Turn the page.

Answer the questions below.

1 **What was the big idea in this story?**

- ◯ Don't believe everything you hear.
- ◯ Practice helps you do well.
- ◯ Things don't go well when you feel sick.
- ◯ It is important to be sure of yourself.

2 **What was the *last* thing that happened in this story?**

- ◯ Gene and his dad practiced piano.
- ◯ Gene heard his name called.
- ◯ Gene wasn't nervous anymore.
- ◯ It was Gene's turn to play.

3 **What did Gene *probably* do just after he played the piano in the contest?**

- ◯ took another turn
- ◯ called his dad
- ◯ went back to his seat
- ◯ went home

4 **What do you think Gene and his dad most likely did after the contest?**

Name ____

Read the selection. Then answer the questions that follow.

The Backyard Party

Angie and Gina wanted to have a party because school was almost over for the summer. They wanted to invite all their friends, but their houses were too small for so many people. Gina thought that her big backyard would be perfect for the party, so she asked her mom if she could have the party there. Gina's mom agreed, so the girls began to make plans for the best party ever.

First, Angie and Gina made a list of their friends. Then they made fancy invitations that told the time and place of the party. Next, Angie began writing names on the cards, while Gina made a list of food to buy. Because the weather was warm, Gina wanted to have ice cream for dessert.

"What games should we play?" Angie asked.

"Let's play the ring-toss game that we played last summer," Gina said.

Just then Gina's mom came into the room. "What's the date of the party?" she asked.

Gina and Angie looked at each other and laughed. They had been so busy making plans for the party that they'd forgotten to pick a day for it!

Turn the page.

Answer the questions below.

1 **What do you think Gina and Angie will do next?**

- ○ plan a beginning of the school year party
- ○ pick a day for the party
- ○ give Gina's mom a list of food to buy
- ○ practice the ring-toss game

2 **What clue words tell you the sequence of events in the second paragraph?**

- ○ made, began
- ○ first, then, next
- ○ told, because
- ○ time, place

3 **What did you learn about people from this story?**

- ○ When people work together, they sometimes disagree.
- ○ People who are busy enjoy life much more.
- ○ When people are excited, they can forget things.
- ○ People around the world celebrate differently.

4 **Which of the following happened first?**

- ○ Gina got permission to have the party.
- ○ Angie and Gina made invitations.
- ○ Gina's mom asked about the date of the party.
- ○ Gina and Angie made a list of friends to invite.

5 **If you were planning a party, what would you do first, second, and third?**

Name ______________________________

Read the selection. Then answer the questions that follow.

Henry's New Bed

My cat Henry could sleep almost anywhere and anytime. Sometimes I found him curled up in an armchair, or sleeping on a pile of clothes, or napping in my bed. One day my mom told me that it was time for Henry to have a bed of his own.

"Carl, you should make a bed for Henry," Mom said. "I'll help you."

First, we looked for a basket in the basement and found an old laundry basket that we didn't use anymore. Next, we needed something soft for Henry to sleep on. I suggested my pillow, but Mom didn't think that was a good idea. She found some old towels and put them in the basket. I wanted to show the bed to Henry right away, but Mom said that we should put one of his favorite toys in the basket first. I found Henry's toy mouse and put it in the basket.

"Now we need to find a place to put Henry's bed," Mom said.

We decided to put Henry's bed on the floor near my bed. When I showed Henry his new bed, he jumped right in, turned around a few times, and then quickly fell asleep. From then on, we found him in his own bed more often than in mine.

Turn the page.

Answer the questions below.

1 **What happened right *after* Mom and Carl found the basket for Henry?**

- ◯ Henry jumped into the basket.
- ◯ Carl found Henry's toy.
- ◯ Carl found a place for the basket.
- ◯ Mom found some towels.

2 **What was the theme in this story?**

- ◯ Cats are easier to take care of than dogs.
- ◯ Cats like to sleep in their own beds.
- ◯ Cats like real mice better than toy mice.
- ◯ Cats sleep more than people do.

3 **Henry saw his new bed for the first time right *after* Mom and Carl**

- ◯ put the towels in the basket.
- ◯ found a basket.
- ◯ looked for a basket.
- ◯ found a place for the bed.

4 **Why was it important to put one of Henry's favorite toys in the basket *before* showing him his new bed?**

____

____

____

____

____

____

5 **What are the clue words that tell you the sequence of events in this story?**

____

____

____

____

____

Name ______________________________________

Read the selection. Then answer the questions that follow.

Makoto's Garden

Every day after school, Makoto helped her grandmother in the garden. One day Makoto asked her grandmother if she could have a plant of her own.

Grandmother smiled and said, "First, get a pot and fill it with dirt from the shed."

Makoto came back with a pot filled with dirt. "What's next?" she asked.

Grandmother showed Makoto some packages of seeds.

"What do you want to grow?" she asked.

Makoto chose the tomato seeds. Then her grandmother showed her how to bury the seeds in the dirt and gently water them.

"Now the pot needs to get some sun," said Grandmother.

Turn the page.

Answer the questions below.

1 **When did Makoto plant her seds?**

- ○ after she watered them
- ○ after she put the dirt in the pot
- ○ after she put the pot in the sun
- ○ before she got the dirt from the shed

2 **How can you tell that Makoto liked gardening?**

- ○ She liked tomatoes.
- ○ She knew how to plant seeds.
- ○ She asked for her own plant.
- ○ She played outside after school.

3 **If the pot of seeds gets enough sun and water, what will happen *next*?**

- ○ It will be time for school.
- ○ Grandmother will be angry at Makoto.
- ○ Tomato plants will start to grow.
- ○ Makoto will fill the pot with dirt.

4 **From this story, what can you tell about Makoto's grandmother?**

Name ______________________________________

Read the selection. Then answer the questions that follow.

The New Shoes

When Kimberly came home, her mother said, "I have something for you."

"Wow! What is it?" Kimberly asked excitedly.

Mom drew a pair of new red shoes from behind her back.

"They are beautiful!" said Kimberly. "Thanks, Mom!" Kimberly had wanted new shoes to go with the new dress her grandma had given her for her upcoming violin recital.

Kimberly sat down at the kitchen table to try on the new shoes. She pushed her right foot slowly into the shoe. "Ouch!" she exclaimed. "That pinches. These shoes are too tight."

"That's not possible," Mom said. "They are the same size as your other shoes. Let me have a look."

Mom inspected the new shoes. "You're right, Kimberly. These don't fit well."

"Can we go to the mall right now to get bigger ones?" Kimberly asked.

"Not now, Kimberly. I have to make dinner. We can go tomorrow after school, okay?"

"Okay, I can wait."

"Silly me," said Mom, "buying you shoes without having you try them on first!"

"Don't worry," said Kimberly. "Tomorrow we can exchange them for the right size, and I can use them next week at my violin recital. I'm so thrilled."

Turn the page.

Answer the questions below.

1 What happened *first* in this story?

- ○ Mom gave Kimberly some new shoes.
- ○ Kimberly tried on the new shoes.
- ○ Kimberly came home from school.
- ○ Mom said she had to make dinner.

2 Where did this story take place?

- ○ at the shoe store
- ○ at Kimberly's house
- ○ at a violin recital
- ○ at Kimberly's school

3 What happened *right after* Kimberly said the shoes were too tight?

- ○ Mom took a closer look at them.
- ○ Mom said they could go to the store.
- ○ Kimberly told Mom not to worry.
- ○ Mom showed Kimberly a new dress.

4 What did Kimberly do that showed you she was patient?

- ○ She tried on the new pair of red shoes again.
- ○ She told her mother the shoes were too small.
- ○ She asked her mother if they could go to the store.
- ○ She said she could wait to go get bigger shoes.

5 What would have been the best order of events to buy Kimberly new shoes? Write the events in order from 1 to 4.

Name ____

Read the selection. Then answer the questions that follow.

Basketball Practice

Benny and Derrick walked to the gym together for basketball practice as they did every Saturday morning. There they found a note from Coach Saba taped to the door. The note said that the coach had been called away and that practice would begin one hour late.

Benny and Derrick did not want to walk all the way back home, so they walked to the bookstore instead. When they got there, the store was closed. They started walking back to the gym, but on the way they met Rafael. The three friends decided to walk to the park.

After walking through the park, the boys headed back toward the gym. On the way, they met Erica who was going to the library. The four friends walked to the library together.

When Benny and Derrick finally got back to the gym, Coach Saba was waiting for them.

"OK, we're going to warm up by running around the gym," he said.

"Oh, no," said Benny. "I feel as if I already ran around the gym at least twice."

And the two friends began to laugh.

Turn the page.

Answer the questions below.

1 **What was the *first* thing Benny and Derrick did in this story?**

- ◯ found the note from Coach Saba
- ◯ met Rafael
- ◯ walked to the gym
- ◯ went to the bookstore

2 **What will Benny and Derrick *probably* do now?**

- ◯ run around the gym
- ◯ say hello to Erica
- ◯ wait for the coach to get there
- ◯ walk home

3 **Why did Benny feel as if he had already run around the gym?**

- ◯ He was upset that practice started late.
- ◯ He had been to the library.
- ◯ He had gotten up early.
- ◯ He had been walking for an hour.

4 **Describe the setting of this story.**

____

____

____

____

____

____

5 **Tell what Erica *most likely* did at the library. Use sequence words in your answer.**

____

____

____

____

____

Name ____

Read the selection. Then answer the questions that follow.

Frogs and Toads

Frogs and toads are the same in some ways. They are different in other ways. Both creatures are found all over the world.

Both frogs and toads begin their lives in water. Later they live on land.

Frogs have smooth skin that is wet. Toads have bumpy skin that is dry. Frogs have teeth, but toads do not. Frogs have long legs that can jump far. Toads have short legs. They mostly walk. Frogs lay eggs in groups. Toads lay eggs in long chains.

Both frogs and toads are fun creatures to study.

Turn the page.

Answer the questions below.

1 **Which sentence from the selection is a statement of opinion?**

○ Both creatures are found all over the world.
○ Both frogs and toads are fun creatures to study.
○ Frogs and toads are the same in some ways.
○ They are different in other ways.

2 **How are frogs and toads alike?**

○ They both have short legs.
○ They both mostly walk.
○ They both are born in water.
○ They both jump well.

3 **In what way are frogs and toads different?**

○ how they lay their eggs
○ where they live as adults
○ how they are seen everywhere
○ where they start life

4 **What are two ways that a frog's skin is different from a toad's skin?**

Name ______________________________

Read the selection. Then answer the questions that follow.

Foxes and Wolves

Foxes and wolves both belong to the Canid family, like pet dogs. Their similarities and differences are interesting.

Both are furry mammals with long noses and ears that stand up. Foxes are often red or black. Wolves are white, gray, or black.

Wolves are large, about the size of large pet dogs. Foxes are small, only a little larger than pet cats.

Foxes and wolves both eat meat. Wolves hunt large animals, such as deer and moose. Foxes hunt small animals, such as rabbits and squirrels. Foxes will eat other food, too, that wolves do not eat, such as fruits, plants, and even garbage.

Wolves live and hunt in packs. A pack usually has six to eight wolves. Foxes usually live alone, but they do mate to have young.

Wolves need a lot of room to roam. They range over hundreds of miles. Foxes stay within just a few miles.

Sadly, many wolves have been killed off. They live today in the coldest, most remote parts of the country. Foxes, on the other hand, have spread. They live in deserts, forests, and even big cities.

Turn the page.

Answer the questions below.

1 **What is one way that foxes are different from wolves?**

- ◯ Foxes have long noses.
- ◯ Foxes eat meat.
- ◯ Foxes live on their own.
- ◯ Foxes hunt for their food.

2 **Which of these is a statement of opinion?**

- ◯ They range over hundreds of miles.
- ◯ Their similarities and differences are interesting.
- ◯ Foxes are often red or black.
- ◯ A pack usually has six to eight wolves.

3 **How are foxes and wolves alike?**

- ◯ They both are related to pet dogs.
- ◯ They both are being killed off.
- ◯ They both want to eat large animals.
- ◯ They both are very small mammals.

4 **The author compares foxes to all of these *except***

- ◯ pet dogs.
- ◯ pet cats.
- ◯ wolves.
- ◯ squirrels.

5 **Foxes may live in big cities, but wolves do not. Compare and contrast the reasons why foxes can live in cities but not wolves.**

Name ______________________________

Read the selection. Then answer the questions that follow.

Moths and Butterflies

Most children adore butterflies. Girls often wear butterfly pins in their hair. Artists use butterflies to decorate objects. Moths do not have nearly so many fans. Have you ever seen anyone wearing a moth pin? There are good reasons to appreciate moths, however.

In some ways, moths and butterflies are alike. Both moths and butterflies are flying insects. If you look closely, you will notice that moths have bigger, furry bodies. Butterflies have thin, hairless bodies. Young moths and butterflies are both like worms, and they change and grow wings later on.

Butterflies are generally more colorful than moths, but moths have other interesting traits. The silkworm is a moth that makes thread people can use to produce fabric. The Atlas moth does that too, and it is enormous. This moth measures up to twelve inches across!

Butterflies are more active during the day, when they can easily be seen. You need to look for moths at night instead, and that is fun. Moths fly toward light, so bring out your flashlight!

Girls should decorate their hair styles with moth pins. Then maybe children would start to love moths too.

Turn the page.

Answer the questions below.

1 **Which clue word in this sentence tells you that it is a statement of opinion?**

Girls should decorate their hair styles with moth pins.

- ◯ girls
- ◯ should
- ◯ styles
- ◯ pins

2 **The author compares young moths and butterflies to**

- ◯ worms.
- ◯ pins.
- ◯ eggs.
- ◯ babies.

3 **How are butterflies and moths alike?**

- ◯ They both are very popular with children.
- ◯ They both gain wings later in life.
- ◯ They both are used in making cloth.
- ◯ They both fly around a lot at night.

4 **How are moths and butterflies different in the way they look?**

____

____

____

____

____

5 **What is one way you can tell that people like butterflies more than moths?**

____

____

____

____

____

Name ______________________________________

Read the selection. Then answer the questions that follow.

The Best Picture Wins

Enter Kid City's new Photo Contest! You and your family could win a trip to Water World!

Just fill out the form on the next page and send in your photo by May 15. One week later, we will pick the winner.

Enter as many pictures as you want. Pay two dollars for each picture you send.

Before you send in your entry, your parent must sign the form.

Do not wait! Enter now!

(Contest is for children 8–12 years old only. Children who have won prizes before may not enter again.)

Turn the page.

Answer the questions below.

1 **Why do you think the author wrote this selection?**

- ◯ to explain how to take pictures
- ◯ to inform readers about a water park
- ◯ to get readers to enter a contest
- ◯ to tell a story about a kid in the city

2 **What should you do *before* you send in your entry?**

- ◯ Wait a week to hear who wins.
- ◯ Show the form to your teacher.
- ◯ Win a fun trip for your family.
- ◯ Get your parent to sign the form.

3 **Why did the author include a date in this selection?**

- ◯ to show how long ago it was written
- ◯ to tell when the form must be sent in
- ◯ to show when a picture was taken
- ◯ to tell how old children must be

4 **Why do you think the author included the sentences "Do not wait! Enter now!" in this selection?**

Name ___________________________________

Read the selection. Then answer the questions that follow.

Chatty Charlie

Charlie Chipmunk loved to talk. When Charlie got to school in the morning, he told his friends about his pet cat. In the afternoon, Charlie told everyone about his favorite soccer team. Charlie also liked to answer Mr. Owl's questions even when Mr. Owl had asked other students to answer.

Charlie's teacher called Charlie's mom and dad. "Can you help me stop Charlie from talking so much?" he asked.

Mr. Chipmunk had an idea. He told Charlie, "Put this rubber band on your wrist. Then when you feel like talking, pull it instead."

The next day Charlie was surprised. It seemed as if he was pulling the rubber band all day! On the second day, Charlie didn't pull it as much. On the third day, Charlie hardly pulled the rubber band at all.

Now Charlie didn't do all the talking. When the teacher asked a question, Charlie let other students answer. Charlie listened to his friends' stories instead of always telling his own stories.

"You did it, and we're proud of you, Charlie," said his mom and dad. "You can take the rubber band off now."

"I think I'll keep it on to remind myself to be quiet. But not all the time," Charlie said and laughed.

Turn the page.

Answer the questions below.

1 **What is the author's main purpose in the *first* paragraph?**

- ◯ to tell readers about Charlie's pet cat
- ◯ to show how much Charlie talked
- ◯ to describe Charlie's grades in school
- ◯ to explain about Charlie's soccer team

2 **What happened *after* Charlie started using the rubber band?**

- ◯ Mr. Owl called Charlie's parents.
- ◯ Charlie's dad came up with a plan.
- ◯ Mr. Chipmunk explained his idea.
- ◯ Charlie stopped doing all the talking.

3 **How do you think the author wants you to feel about Charlie at the *end* of the story?**

- ◯ proud
- ◯ angry
- ◯ sorry
- ◯ quiet

4 **What is the author's main purpose in the *last* paragraph?**

- ◯ to show that Charlie is afraid to talk any more
- ◯ to remind readers they should be quiet all the time
- ◯ to show that Charlie is glad he learned this lesson
- ◯ to explain using rubber bands to break bad habits

5 **What are two likely reasons why the author wrote this story?**

____

____

____

____

____

____

____

____

Name ______________________________

Read the selection. Then answer the questions that follow.

Glue Through the Ages

If you broke a clay pot today, you would probably fix it with some glue. What did people do thousands of years ago? Did they just throw the pot away? No! People in ancient times had glue too.

The first glue was probably made from tree sap. Archaeologists have discovered clay pots mended with this kind of glue in an ancient burial site. These pots were repaired over 6,000 years ago.

Three thousand years ago, the ancient Greeks made glue to use with wood, tiles, and paper. They used many different kinds of materials to make glue, such as egg whites, milk, cheese, vegetables, grains, and bones. All these things had to be cooked down for a long time until they got sticky.

In 1750, a man in England first patented a type of glue made from fish. This fish glue was used in furniture and paintings. For years, people made glue from animal skins too.

In the twenty-first century, people manufacture glue out of plastic. We can get hot glue, cold glue, gel glue, and even glues that work underwater. How would we hold everything together and survive without glue?

Turn the page.

Answer the questions below.

1 **What is the author's purpose in the *first* paragraph?**

- ◯ to encourage readers to fix things
- ◯ to get readers curious about glue
- ◯ to tell about the life of an inventor
- ◯ to describe the best way to use glue

2 **How do you think the author wants you to feel when reading this selection?**

- ◯ careless
- ◯ puzzled
- ◯ sticky
- ◯ interested

3 **Which kind of glue was made *last*?**

- ◯ fish glue
- ◯ plastic glue
- ◯ plant glue
- ◯ skin glue

4 **What do you think are two reasons that the author wrote this selection?**

____

____

____

____

____

____

5 **Why do you think the author writes about events from the past up to the present?**

____

____

____

____

____

Name ______________________________

Read the selection. Then answer the questions that follow.

Dogs with Jobs

Dogs make good pets. Many dogs have special jobs too.

Dogs have a very good sense of smell. This means they can help find people who are lost.

Some dogs are trained to help people who can't hear. For example, some dogs are trained to alert their owners who cannot hear that a phone is ringing. The dogs become good friends to the people they help.

Dogs also cheer up older people who may be lonely. People often feel happy when they can pet a dog.

Dogs work hard every day. They make life easier for many people.

Turn the page.

Answer the questions below.

1 **What is the main idea of this selection?**

- ◯ Dogs make good pets and do many jobs.
- ◯ People need dogs to help them every day.
- ◯ Only dogs with good hearing and sight can be trained.
- ◯ Dogs cheer up people who are older or lonely.

2 **How is a dog that cheers up a lonely person like a dog that points out a ringing telephone?**

- ◯ They both are trained to do the same things.
- ◯ They both are trained to find things.
- ◯ They both act like house pets.
- ◯ They both are helpful to people.

3 **What is the main idea of the second paragraph?**

- ◯ A dog's sense of smell helps it to find missing people.
- ◯ Dogs have a very good sense of sight.
- ◯ Dogs are trained to find missing people.
- ◯ When people get lost, a dog can find them.

4 **What would be another good title for this selection?**

Name ____

Read the selection. Then answer the questions that follow.

The Real Dr. Seuss

You have probably heard of Dr. Seuss. Have you heard of Theodor Seuss Geisel? Ted Geisel used the name Dr. Seuss when he wrote *The Cat in the Hat* and *Green Eggs and Ham.*

Ted Geisel did not start out as a children's author. At first, he wrote for adults. He also drew cartoons. On a trip in 1937, Ted Geisel wrote his first book as Dr. Seuss. He used the name Seuss because it was his middle name. He used the title of Dr. because his father wanted him to be a doctor.

In 1954, Ted's boss read an article about problems children were having learning to read. The article said that children's books were boring. Ted's boss gave him a challenge. Could he write a book children would enjoy using only 250 words? Nine months later, Ted gave his boss *The Cat in the Hat.* The book used only 220 words. It was an instant success.

In 1960, Ted was given another challenge. Could he write a children's book using only 50 words? Yes, *Green Eggs and Ham* was the happy result.

When Ted Geisel died in 1991, he had written more than 44 books. More than 200 million copies had found their way into homes and hearts around the world.

Turn the page.

Answer the questions below.

1 What is this selection *mostly* about?

- ○ how Dr. Seuss wrote *Green Eggs and Ham*
- ○ why children have trouble reading
- ○ the man who wrote the Dr. Seuss books
- ○ why Dr. Seuss used so few words in his books

2 Which of these would *not* be a supporting detail for this selection?

- ○ Ted Geisel was born in Springfield, Massachusetts, in 1904.
- ○ Dr. Seuss also wrote *How the Grinch Stole Christmas.*
- ○ Dr. Seuss was not a great poet.
- ○ Dr. Seuss's books have been translated into more than 15 languages.

3 How were the Dr. Seuss books different from other children's books of that time?

- ○ His books were not about animals.
- ○ The other books were fun to read.
- ○ His books were boring and hard to read.
- ○ The other books used many more words.

4 What is the main idea of the first paragraph?

- ○ Dr. Seuss read about children learning to read.
- ○ Dr. Seuss's real name was Theodor Seuss Geisel.
- ○ Theodor Geisel was a successful children's author.
- ○ Ted Geisel first wrote for adults, not children.

5 Why do you think the author called this selection "The Real Dr. Seuss"?

____

____

____

____

____

____

____

____

Name ______________________________

Read the selection. Then answer the questions that follow.

Flying Dragons?

Have you ever seen a dragon fly? Maybe not, but if you are near a pond in the summer, you may see an insect called a dragonfly. Even though their name makes them sound fierce, dragonflies do not harm people. In fact, people are happy to see them because they eat other insects that people do not like.

These small, thin, winged insects have been around for more than 300 million years. They are born under the water, grow up in the water, and live in the air for only one or two months.

Most people learn to identify dragonflies by their wings, which shimmer in colors such as green, purple, and blue. Their wings are stronger than they look, carrying the dragonflies at about sixty miles an hour. That's about as fast as a car on a highway.

Every year millions of dragonflies move from place to place, always settling near water. It is a stunning sight.

If you are lucky enough to see these striking insects this summer, you can thank them for being such beautiful and helpful friends.

Turn the page.

Answer the questions below.

1 **What is the topic of this selection?**

- ◯ insects
- ◯ dragonflies
- ◯ flying dragons
- ◯ nature

2 **What is the main idea of this selection?**

- ◯ Dragonflies are small, thin, winged insects.
- ◯ Scientists do not know why dragonflies settle near water.
- ◯ Dragonflies are helpful and beautiful insects.
- ◯ Dragonflies have been around for 300 million years.

3 **How are dragonflies different from other insects?**

- ◯ Dragonflies are more fierce and harmful.
- ◯ Dragonflies only live in the water.
- ◯ People have trouble identifying dragonflies.
- ◯ People find dragonflies helpful.

4 **What are two supporting details from the first paragraph?**

____

____

____

____

____

____

5 **What is the main idea of the third paragraph?**

____

____

____

____

____

Name ______________________________________

Read the selection. Then answer the questions that follow.

The Cards

Bae and Hana were making cards for Mother's Day. Hana put some paper and stickers on the kitchen table.

"We need crayons too!" Bae said. "Did you forget again, little sister?"

"Me, forget?" said Hana, laughing back at him. "This morning, you left your glasses in the hall. That was silly, my older and wiser brother."

"Let's stop teasing and get to work," said Bae. He took a blue crayon and started drawing a flower.

"I wanted to make Mom a flower!" Hana protested.

"So?" said Bae. "She can get two flower cards."

"OK," said Hana, taking a red crayon. "Mom will like *mine* better, I'm sure."

Turn the page.

Answer the questions below.

1 **What happens at the *beginning* of the story?**

- ○ Bae and Hana buy stickers.
- ○ Bae loses his glasses.
- ○ Hana forgets the crayons.
- ○ Bae and Hana draw flowers.

2 **What is one way that Hana and Bae are different in this story?**

- ○ They choose different colored crayons.
- ○ They make cards for different people.
- ○ They draw pictures of different things.
- ○ They use different kinds of paper.

3 **How will Bae and Hana's cards look the same?**

- ○ Both cards will be large.
- ○ Both cards will be messy.
- ○ Both cards will have flowers.
- ○ Both cards will have words.

4 **What is one way that Bae and Hana are alike in this story? Explain your answer.**

Name ___________________________________

Read the selection. Then answer the questions that follow.

Moving Time

It was time for Ayasha's family to close up their summer camp. All summer they had lived in the woods in their little round hut. It had a bent wood frame and was lined with bark from birch trees. Ayasha had played outside most days. She had fished and swum and made toys from leaves and pebbles and sticks.

Now she and the others would move back to their winter cabin in the town beside the river. The winter cabin was a rectangular building made from flat planks of wood just like the Europeans used. Ayasha's people were Ojibwe. They moved each season to a new home. The Europeans stayed in town all year. She did not know why they did that—it seemed so boring—but that was what they did.

Ayasha helped pack up her family's belongings. She was sad the summer was over. Soon all the wonderful colors would be gone, and all she would see was white, grey, brown, and black. How awful! Winter was so cold. It was like a mean trader, she thought, who would not give free candy even to a child. She wished there were a way she could make summer last forever.

Turn the page.

Answer the questions below.

1 **Why does Ayasha's family have to move?**

- ○ The hut had gotten too small.
- ○ There were no more fish in the river.
- ○ The Europeans were taking the land.
- ○ The summer was coming to an end.

2 **How are the Europeans different from the Ojibwe in this story?**

- ○ They live in rectangular wooden buildings.
- ○ They remain in the town all year around.
- ○ They build their homes from flat planks.
- ○ They have homes in the town beside the river.

3 **In this story, the author compares winter to**

- ○ a mean trader.
- ○ free candy.
- ○ birch trees.
- ○ a small child.

4 **How did Ayasha think that the summer was different from the winter?**

- ○ The Ojibwe family stayed in the town all year long.
- ○ The Europeans moved to a new home each season.
- ○ The summer colors were better than the winter colors.
- ○ Her summer toys were more fun than her winter toys.

5 **In what three ways are the winter cabin and the summer hut different?**

Name ____________________________________

Read the selection. Then answer the questions that follow.

Corey's Lesson

Corey sat at his desk staring at his closed science textbook. "I don't care if I fail the stupid test," he muttered to himself. Just then Dan walked into the room.

"Dan, why do I need to know about the rain forest anyway?" Corey asked his older brother. Corey and Dan were friends as well as brothers. They shared many of the same interests. Corey especially liked to go bike riding with Dan because Dan knew all the best biking trails.

Dan thought about Corey's question. "You have to study about the rain forest so that you can learn how to protect it," he said.

"Why does it need to be protected?" Corey asked.

"In a lot of ways, it can't protect itself," Dan said. "And the animals and plants that live there are in danger of dying out completely. So if they no longer exist, we can't learn from them or use them."

Corey was surprised because he didn't know that some animals were in danger of becoming extinct. Now he was more interested in learning about the rain forest.

"I'll make a deal with you," Dan said. "You study for an hour, and then I'll go bike riding with you. We'll go on that special trail I was telling you about."

"It's a deal," said Corey eagerly as he opened his book.

Turn the page.

Answer the questions below.

1 **Which of these is *not* important to the plot of this story?**

- ◯ Corey is sitting at his desk.
- ◯ Corey asks Dan about rain forests.
- ◯ Dan promises to take Corey bike riding later.
- ◯ Dan gives a reason for studying about rain forests.

2 **How are Corey and Dan alike?**

- ◯ They both dislike taking tests.
- ◯ They both like to ride bikes.
- ◯ They both are studying for tests.
- ◯ They both dislike science class.

3 **How are Dan and Corey different in this story?**

- ◯ Corey is interested in rain forests, and Dan is not.
- ◯ Dan stays in his room, but Corey does not.
- ◯ Corey likes going on new trails, but Dan does not.
- ◯ Dan knows more about the rain forest than Corey.

4 **How are the animals and the plants of the rain forest alike?**

____

____

____

____

____

5 **Contrast how Corey feels at the beginning of the story to how he feels at the end of the story. State how Corey feels and why.**

____

____

____

____

____

Name ______________________________

Read the selection. Then answer the questions that follow.

Rania's Sign

Rania and her sister were helping to clean up the beach. There were lots of bottles and cans in the sand. Rania wanted to get her friends to help too. She decided to make a sign to tell her friends about it.

Clean Up the Beach!

When: Every Saturday morning, 8 A.M.
Where: All-City Beach

Be sure to bring boots and gloves.
Bring garbage bags if you can.

YOU Can Make a Difference!

Help make the beach
a safe place to play.

Rania knew that once her friends read the sign, they would want to help too.

Turn the page.

Answer the questions below.

1 **What is this passage mostly about?**

◯ Rania's Saturday morning

◯ Rania and her sister

◯ Rania's effort to help

◯ Rania, going to the beach

2 **Where would Rania *probably* put her sign?**

◯ at school

◯ on a car

◯ at the train station

◯ on her front door

3 **What do Rania's actions tell you about her?**

◯ She does not work well with others.

◯ She likes to swim in the ocean.

◯ She wants more than her share of things.

◯ She does not think only of herself.

4 **Why does Rania think her friends will want to help too?**

Name ______________________________

Read the selection. Then answer the questions that follow.

Simon's Pets

My friend Simon is lucky. He has a saltwater fish tank with many kinds of fish. The salt water means that Simon can keep tropical fish, the colorful fish that live in the oceans.

Simon's three favorite fish are Annie, Red, and Polly. Annie is a clown fish. She is orange with white wavy stripes on each side. Annie is shy and likes to hide near the "live rocks" at the bottom of the tank. Simon says that the live rocks are like living filters that keep the water clean.

Red is a flame angel fish. He is bright red with black bands on each side. Whenever Simon comes near the tank, Red comes to the side because he thinks he will get something to eat.

I like Polly the most. She is orange with bright green squiggly lines all over her. Simon says that he can have only one of these fish in the tank at a time. Simon doesn't know why, but that's what his fish book says.

Simon and I like to spend time watching the fish and reading about how to take care of them. It's my favorite hobby too.

Turn the page.

Answer the questions below.

1 **What is this passage mostly about?**

- ◯ fish that live in the ocean
- ◯ how to care for a fish tank
- ◯ Simon's fish tank
- ◯ Simon's best friend

2 **What can you tell about Simon by the way he treats his pets?**

- ◯ He likes to solve puzzles.
- ◯ He is a good student.
- ◯ He is greedy.
- ◯ He is responsible.

3 **What is one thing Simon likes about tropical fish?**

- ◯ their bright colors
- ◯ the food they eat
- ◯ the way they feel
- ◯ the way they sound

4 **What do you think might happen if the tank had no "live rocks"?**

- ◯ Some of the fish would become less colorful.
- ◯ The water would lose some of its salt.
- ◯ The fish would have no place to hide.
- ◯ The water would become dirty.

5 **What are three things Simon needs to know about his pets?**

Name ___________________________________

Read the selection. Then answer the questions that follow.

Work Not Play

Children in Colonial America lived different lives from children today. They did not go to school; however, their lives were not all about fun. Their parents taught them to obey and how to do farm work and house work. The children's work was important to their families.

Girls cooked and baked, sewed, and gathered herbs for medicine. They ground grains like corn and barley into flour. For their baking, they measured the flour with their hands. They cooked in fireplaces instead of ovens. The girls learned all kinds of sewing stitches and how to mend clothes. They spun wool and knit clothing as well.

Boys hunted, planted and harvested crops, and took care of the farm animals. They woke up at dawn to fetch water in buckets from a spring and feed the animals. They weeded the gardens and chased birds away from the seed. They also gathered reeds for roofing and made wooden fences and tools.

Children in those days did have some fun too. They played with corn husk dolls and wooden toys. Still, most of their days were taken up with hard work. Imagine if you had to live back then!

Turn the page.

Answer the questions below.

1 **What is the *third* paragraph mainly about?**

- ◯ girls doing house work
- ◯ boys going to school
- ◯ girls playing games
- ◯ boys doing farm work

2 **What can you conclude about the girls and boys described in this selection?**

- ◯ They did different kinds of work.
- ◯ They learned to read in school.
- ◯ They were not kept very busy.
- ◯ They got paid for the work they did.

3 **The author writes, "For their baking, they measured the flour with their hands." You can conclude from this that**

- ◯ they did not bake pies or cakes.
- ◯ they did not use measuring cups.
- ◯ their breads did not come out right.
- ◯ they measured water with a spoon.

4 **How do you think the children described in the selection felt about their free time? Explain your answer.**

____

____

____

____

5 **Tell two ways that your life would have been different if you had lived in those times instead of today. Explain your answer.**

____

____

____

____

____

Name ______________________________________

Read the selection. Then answer the questions that follow.

The Disappearing Pile of Leaves

It was a beautiful fall day. Dad and I were raking leaves into a big pile. My dog Penny was chasing leaves as they fell off the trees. Dad and I were cold, so we went into the house to make some hot chocolate. When we went back outside, the pile of leaves was gone! We started making another pile. Soon, Mom called us in for lunch. When we went back outside to finish our job, the pile was gone again!

Dad laughed and petted Penny. He said, "Before we start another pile, let's put Penny in the house."

The next pile of leaves did not disappear.

Turn the page.

Answer the questions below.

1 **Why do you think the author wrote this story?**

- ◯ to explain how to rake leaves
- ◯ to share information about dogs
- ◯ to make the reader smile
- ◯ to describe a beautiful fall day

2 **How is the last pile of leaves different from the first two piles?**

- ◯ Dad does not help make the last pile.
- ◯ Penny does not ruin the last pile.
- ◯ The last pile has fewer leaves in it.
- ◯ Mom helps with making the last pile.

3 **How does the author want you to feel about the job of raking leaves?**

- ◯ that it is fun
- ◯ that it is a hard job
- ◯ that it cannot be done
- ◯ that it has to be done fast

4 **How does the author tell you how Dad feels about Penny?**

Name ___________________________________

Read the selection. Then answer the questions that follow.

Eduardo's Seashells

Eduardo is a "sheller." That's the name for a person who picks up seashells. He lives in Florida, so there are many beaches where he can look for shells that have washed up on the shore. All he needs is a pail and some shoes to protect his feet. He also reads books about shells so that he can learn their names.

Eduardo has many ideas about how to display his shells. He puts some shells around a picture frame. With his mother's help, he makes holes in some shells and puts them on a string. His mother thinks the shells look like jewels, and she likes to wear them around her neck. Eduardo gives some shells to his friends. They use them to make their fish tanks look more natural.

Eduardo's favorite idea for the shells is to fasten them to pieces of wood he finds on the beach. He hangs these pieces on the wall in his room. He likes to lie on his bed and look at them.

Eduardo knows that there are many more ideas for using shells, but he already has a good start.

Turn the page.

Answer the questions below.

1 **Why do you think the author wrote this selection?**

- ◯ to persuade the reader to collect seashells
- ◯ to inform the reader about different ways to use shells
- ◯ to express feelings about seashells and "shellers"
- ◯ to describe the best way to look for seashells

2 **Eduardo's favorite idea for shells is different from his other ideas because**

- ◯ He hangs the shells on his wall instead of giving them away.
- ◯ He uses the shells in fish tanks rather than for crafts.
- ◯ He paints the shells instead of gluing them on picture frames.
- ◯ He has the shells displayed at school rather than at home.

3 **Why did the author say that Eduardo only needs a pail and some shoes?**

- ◯ to show that Eduardo was serious about seashells
- ◯ to show that Eduardo was not prepared to collect shells
- ◯ to show that you should protect yourself on the beach
- ◯ to show that collecting shells is not an expensive hobby

4 **Why do you think the author compares shells on a string to jewels?**

- ◯ to make shells seem like art
- ◯ to show that shells can be expensive
- ◯ to show how beautiful shells can be
- ◯ to explain that shells are easy to find

5 **Name two things that the author wants you to know about Eduardo.**

Name ___________________________________

Read the selection. Then answer the questions that follow.

Totem Poles

If you have studied about America, you have probably read about totem poles. The first totem poles were made by Native Americans who lived near the Pacific Ocean.

The totem poles were tall poles made from redwood trees. A skilled artist carved people, animals, and make-believe creatures into the poles. Long ago, the Native Americans did not have a written language. The carvings on the poles were used to explain how the Native American tribes lived and what was important to them. The carvings also described the myths and legends of a particular tribe.

A ceremony marked the raising of a totem pole. A hole was dug, and the pole was nested in it. Because the poles were large and heavy, the raising process required many people with ropes. During the raising ceremony, a speaker explained the details and stories behind the carvings. The people of the tribe listened to and remembered the stories so that the stories could be passed down.

Learning about totem poles helps you understand what was important to other people. It might also inspire you to think about what is important to you.

Turn the page.

Answer the questions below.

1 **Why do you think the author wrote this selection?**

- ◯ to persuade students to study American history
- ◯ to express feelings about the history of Native Americans
- ◯ to describe the Native Americans who lived by the ocean
- ◯ to explain a Native American custom

2 **What is the author's purpose in the last paragraph?**

- ◯ to interest the reader to learn more
- ◯ to inform the reader about the purpose of totem poles
- ◯ to encourage the reader to admire Native American culture
- ◯ to persuade the reader to protect historic totem poles

3 **The author thinks that using the carvings on the totem poles is *most* like**

- ◯ wearing animal face masks.
- ◯ raising heavy redwood trees.
- ◯ having a written language.
- ◯ listening to make-believe creatures.

4 **What is the author's purpose in the third paragraph?**

____

____

____

____

____

5 **Why does the author tell you about the importance of totem poles?**

____

____

____

____

____

____

Name ___________________________________

Read the selection. Then answer the questions that follow.

A New Girl in Class

Keiko is a new girl in school. She moved here from Japan. She is learning to speak English.

Our class is learning about people from other countries. Our teacher told us to choose a country and find pictures of that country and its people to share with the class.

One day, Keiko surprised the class. She came to school wearing a bright blue dress called a kimono. It was different and beautiful! Then she shared some food from her country. Everyone tasted it. The food was delicious.

That was our most interesting class and the most fun!

Turn the page.

Answer the questions below.

1 **What does this story tell you about Keiko?**

- ◯ She does not like surprises.
- ◯ She likes American food.
- ◯ She is excited to learn English.
- ◯ She is proud of her country.

2 **What is the *second* paragraph all about?**

- ◯ A girl's class studies other countries.
- ◯ A girl has moved here from Japan.
- ◯ A girl's class tries on different outfits.
- ◯ A girl learns about the country of Japan.

3 **What is the main idea of the *third* paragraph?**

- ◯ Keiko surprises the class by speaking English.
- ◯ Keiko's stories make all the children nervous.
- ◯ Keiko brings in real things instead of pictures.
- ◯ Keiko's country is very far away from here.

4 **What two things does Keiko bring to class?**

Name ______________________________

Read the selection. Then answer the questions that follow.

It's for the Birds

Sometimes I just do not understand Julie. She loves to watch birds! She has four bird feeders in her yard, and the birds are always flapping around making a lot of clatter. Then Julie and her friends stand around watching and listening to the birds. They won't move or talk because the birds will fly away.

Julie even bought a machine that makes bird sounds. Now it seems as if I hear bird noises coming from inside her house too.

Sometimes her friends from the bird club come to her house to plan new bird-watching trips or to look at pictures of birds from earlier trips. Last year, the club went to a beach in Texas to watch birds for three days. When I asked Julie if she went swimming while she was at the beach, she said that she didn't have time. I just don't understand how she could be at a beach and not go swimming.

Last spring Julie made houses for the birds. I saw the eggs and the baby birds after they hatched. Now there are even more birds!

There are many things I don't understand, but I hope someday to have a hobby like Julie's.

Turn the page.

Answer the questions below.

1 **What is the *first* paragraph all about?**

- ○ Some bird watchers like to use machines to make bird sounds.
- ○ Bird watchers are usually lonely people.
- ○ Some people question how bird watchers can have any fun.
- ○ Bird watchers do not like to move or talk.

2 **With whom does Julie watch birds?**

- ○ a club
- ○ her teacher
- ○ the class
- ○ her family

3 **What does Julie have in her yard?**

- ○ a bird sound machine
- ○ pictures of birds
- ○ bird statues
- ○ bird feeders

4 **At the beach, Julie and her friends did not have time for**

- ○ bird watching.
- ○ swimming.
- ○ having fun.
- ○ taking pictures.

5 **Why do you think someone would like to watch birds?**

___

___

___

___

___

___

___

___

Name ___________________________________

Read the selection. Then answer the questions that follow.

The Spider Catcher

Walter woke up feeling excited because his dad was taking him into the field. His dad was a zoology professor, and today they were hunting for spiders. Most people are afraid of spiders, but not Walter. He has been helping his dad find insects, frogs, and all kinds of creatures since he was a little boy.

Walter put on tall boots and his hat. He grabbed the spider catcher, which looks like a long handle with a brush at one end and a lever on the other end. The spider catcher allows Walter to catch spiders without harming them, and it makes releasing them easy too.

When Walter and his dad got to the field, they walked slowly and looked carefully in the tall grass and under rocks. Dad said that spiders live almost everywhere on Earth, except in very cold places like mountaintops. Spiders even live in holes on beaches.

Walter noticed a web and stopped. He saw a large spider, took out the catcher, and was about to capture the spider when it jumped onto Walter's shirt.

"Be very still," Dad said. "It won't hurt you. It's a jumping spider."

Dad got the spider into a glass dish and closed the cover.

"It looks as if I did not need to buy a spider catcher after all," said Dad as he began to sketch the spider in his notebook.

Turn the page.

Answer the questions below.

1 **What is the *second* paragraph all about?**

- ○ A boy gets ready for a field trip with his dad.
- ○ A boy learns how to use a spider catcher.
- ○ A dad studies spiders and other insects.
- ○ A spider lives almost anywhere on earth.

2 **What is the main idea of the *third* paragraph?**

- ○ Walter hikes up to the mountaintop with his Dad.
- ○ Dad and Walter both draw pictures of spiders.
- ○ Dad teaches Walter where spiders can be found.
- ○ Walter's Dad carries the large spider catcher.

3 **What does Dad use to capture the spider on Walter's shirt?**

- ○ the spider catcher
- ○ the handled brush
- ○ a piece of tissue
- ○ a glass dish

4 **How did Dad know that the jumping spider wouldn't hurt Walter?**

____

____

____

____

____

5 **According to the story, what are good places to hunt for spiders?**

____

____

____

____

____

Name ________________________________

Read the selection. Then answer the questions that follow.

He Had a Dream

Dr. Martin Luther King Jr. had a dream. He grew up when the laws of the United States said that black people and white people were not equal. He knew this was wrong, so he began to work to change the laws.

In 1955, a black woman named Rosa Parks would not give her seat on a city bus to a white man. She went to jail. Dr. King heard about it. He got people to stop riding buses until the law was changed.

In 1963, Dr. King led The March on Washington. Over 200,000 people joined him in this non-violent protest against inequality. In the end, Dr. King's efforts and hard work changed many laws. His dream still lives on today.

Turn the page.

Answer the questions below.

1 **What was Dr. Martin Luther King Jr.'s dream?**

- ◯ He wanted to help white people.
- ◯ People would not break the laws and go to jail.
- ◯ Black people could ride buses.
- ◯ All people would be treated equally someday.

2 **Why did the author write this selection?**

- ◯ to persuade you to stand up on the bus
- ◯ to inform you about a great man
- ◯ to tell a funny story about people
- ◯ to share information about restaurants

3 **Why did black people stop riding buses?**

- ◯ The law said they could do it.
- ◯ They wanted a law to be changed.
- ◯ They did not want to go to jail.
- ◯ They could not afford to pay the fare.

4 **Why was Rosa Parks put in jail for not giving up her seat on the bus?**

Name ___________________________________

Read the selection. Then answer the questions that follow.

A Stormy Day

Gordon watched the summer sky grow darker while his mom and dad prepared for the thunderstorm that was coming. Gordon knew that thunderstorms could be fierce and dangerous. His neighbors had lost part of their roof and some big trees fell over the year before. Gordon's neighbors were lucky because no one got hurt, not even their dog, Bruno.

Gordon heard the wind getting louder and saw the trees bending. Then, he heard thunder in the distance. Soon, a flash of lightning lit up the sky. He was not very worried, though, because his family was well prepared. Gordon had made sure all the water bottles were full in case there was no clean water to drink after the storm. His dad carried enough blankets and pillows to the shelter to keep their family warm and comfortable. His mom brought flashlights, a portable radio, and extra batteries. Just then, they heard rain on the roof.

"Ready to go down?" asked Dad.

When Gordon's family got into their shelter, they turned on the radio. They heard that the storm was not getting stronger and that there was no danger after all. Even though Gordon was safe in the shelter, he was glad to hear the radio announcement.

"Well, we got ready for nothing," Gordon said.

"No," Dad said. "It's always better to be safe than sorry."

Turn the page.

Answer the questions below.

1 **Why did Gordon say that his family got ready for nothing?**

- ◯ because their neighbors didn't need help
- ◯ because the storm was not dangerous
- ◯ because they had enough water bottles
- ◯ because Gordon's family liked storms

2 **Why did they need flashlights, a portable radio, and extra batteries?**

- ◯ because the storm could cause flooding
- ◯ to help walk downstairs
- ◯ in case they lost electric power
- ◯ in case the storm took their roof off

3 **What part of the storm had done the most damage to the neighbors?**

- ◯ the rain
- ◯ the hail
- ◯ the thunder
- ◯ the wind

4 **What was the author's purpose in writing this selection?**

- ◯ to share information about preparing for storms
- ◯ to persuade you to build a shelter in your basement
- ◯ to explain how a family lost the roof of their house
- ◯ to give an opinion about summer thunderstorms

5 **What did it mean when Gordon heard the wind getting louder?**

Name ____________________________________

Read the selection. Then answer the questions that follow.

A Ball of Rock

You are probably not surprised when you see Earth's moon, but you might be surprised by some facts about it.

We know that the moon is about 4.5 billion years old because that is the age of the rocks astronauts brought back from the moon. Most experts believe Earth is about the same age.

Did you know that if you speak on the moon, no one would hear you? On Earth, you can hear sounds because sound travels through air. Since there is no air on the moon, no sounds can be heard. Therefore, when astronauts walked on the moon, they could not hear their footsteps.

Also, because there is no air, the sky is always black on the moon. It is the light traveling through air that makes the sky look blue on Earth.

There is no wind on the moon either. Footprints left on the moon by astronauts will be there for millions of years because there is no wind or air to disturb the footprints.

Scientists once thought that the moon had no water and that nothing could live there. Recently they found frozen water, so scientists now believe it is possible that there may have been life on the moon.

The moon may be an old ball of rock, but without it, our sky would not be nearly as interesting.

Turn the page.

Answer the questions below.

1 **Why did the author write this selection?**

- ◯ to offer an opinion about the Earth's moon
- ◯ to share some interesting facts about the moon
- ◯ to encourage you to look at the moon more often
- ◯ to tell you a story that happened on the moon

2 **What conclusion can you draw from this selection?**

- ◯ The moon would be a good place for humans to live.
- ◯ Earth's moon is very much like Earth.
- ◯ The moon would seem quiet and dark to a human.
- ◯ Life on the moon has never been possible.

3 **What can you conclude about scientists from this selection?**

- ◯ They have learned everything there is to know about the moon.
- ◯ They know how to determine the age of rocks from the moon.
- ◯ They are more interested in learning about Earth than the moon.
- ◯ They have walked around on the moon along with the astronauts.

4 **What is one reason astronauts need to wear spacesuits on the moon?**

____

____

____

____

____

____

5 **Based on the selection, what can you conclude about the frozen water found on the moon?**

____

____

____

____

____

Name ________________________________

Read the selection. Then answer the questions that follow.

Moving Day

Ann's family was getting ready to move to a new house. Ann sat on her bed looking sad. Mom came into Ann's room to help her pack.

"I don't want to move," Ann said.

"I know how you feel," Mom said. "I'm going to miss this house and my friends. I'm nervous because I'll have to make new friends."

Ann was surprised. She hadn't thought that parents would also feel scared about moving. "Don't worry, Mom," she said. "You'll make new friends—just like I will."

"You're right," Mom said. "Thank you for reminding me."

Together, they put Ann's books in boxes and imagined their new friends.

Turn the page.

Answer the questions below.

1 **What happened at the *end* of this story?**

- ○ Ann and her mother packed Ann's books.
- ○ Ann made her mother very nervous.
- ○ Ann and her mother missed their friends.
- ○ Ann's family stayed at their old house.

2 **Where did this story take place?**

- ○ at Ann's new house
- ○ in the back yard
- ○ in the living room
- ○ in Ann's bedroom

3 **How is Ann like her mother?**

- ○ They both were surprised.
- ○ They both enjoyed packing.
- ○ They are both excited about moving.
- ○ They are both nervous about making new friends.

4 **How did Ann's feelings change from the beginning to the end of the story?**

Name ______________________________

Read the selection. Then answer the questions that follow.

Lauren's Busy Day

Lauren had several chores to do every Saturday. But this Saturday was different because Lauren's family was busily preparing for visitors. Lauren had extra things to do too, and she was worried because she couldn't decide what to do first. Lauren's mom told her to make a list and put the jobs on it in order of importance.

First, Lauren decided to write down the things she did every Saturday: put away all her toys and hang up her clothes. So she wrote "clean my room" at the top of her list.

Next, Lauren wrote "clean the fish tank," because it was her job to make sure the fishes' house was clean too.

This week Lauren's additional job was to make an extra bed for her friend who was coming to visit. She wrote "make a bed" next on her list. She planned to make a card that would welcome her friend, so she added "make a card." Lauren was surprised when she realized that having a list made her feel better.

Lauren's mom glanced at the list and wrote "have fun" at the bottom. Lauren laughed and said, "You don't need to write that down because I never forget to have fun."

Turn the page.

Answer the questions below.

1 **How was this Saturday *different* from other Saturdays for Lauren?**

- ◯ She did not want to do her chores.
- ◯ She had more chores to do than usual.
- ◯ She had to put away toys and hang up clothes.
- ◯ She needed to clean the family's fish tank.

2 **Where did this story *probably* take place?**

- ◯ at her friend's house
- ◯ at the pet store
- ◯ at Lauren's house
- ◯ at the card store

3 **Which of these was *not* important to the plot of this story?**

- ◯ Lauren's mom told her to make a list of her jobs.
- ◯ Lauren laughed at what her mom put on the list.
- ◯ Lauren wrote down the things she had to do.
- ◯ Lauren put her jobs in order of their importance.

4 **Why did Lauren's mom write "have fun" at the bottom of the list of chores?**

- ◯ She wanted Lauren to enjoy the day after doing extra chores.
- ◯ She knew Lauren didn't like having visitors.
- ◯ She thought Lauren always forgot to have fun.
- ◯ She knew Lauren didn't like to clean the fish tank.

5 **How did Lauren's feelings change from the beginning to the end of the story?**

Name ___________________________________

Read the selection. Then answer the questions that follow.

Racing with Turtle

In the famous race between Rabbit and Turtle, Rabbit felt sure he would win. That's why he stopped to rest during the race. Turtle was a slow and steady runner, and he won.

Turtle was astonished that he had beaten Rabbit. He knew the reason he had won was not that he ran fast, but that he hadn't stopped once. However, when reporters asked Turtle to explain his win, he replied, "I practiced a lot."

The following day, articles about Turtle appeared in the newspapers. By now he felt extremely important. Rabbit, on the other hand, felt terrible because he knew he was quicker than Turtle. Rabbit's friends tried to cheer him up by saying, "Good things never happen to people who are too proud to do the right thing. Maybe you'll feel better if you call Turtle."

Rabbit called, but Turtle rudely said, "I don't have time to talk."

A month later, Snail invited Turtle to race him. Turtle thought, "Losing is impossible."

Rabbit watched the race, in which Snail was a steadier runner. Rabbit waved to both of them, but only Snail waved back.

Of course, Snail won the race.

Turn the page.

Answer the questions below.

1 **Which of these is *not* important to the plot of the story?**

- ○ Rabbit watched the race between Snail and Turtle.
- ○ Snail won the race against Turtle.
- ○ The newspapers had articles about Turtle's win.
- ○ Turtle beat Rabbit in their race.

2 **Which of these is true about the setting of this story?**

- ○ The story recently happened at a well-known zoo.
- ○ The story occurred during the winter.
- ○ The story happened in a make-believe time and place.
- ○ The story took place all in one day.

3 **Which of these *best* describes the way Snail raced?**

- ○ carelessly
- ○ steadily
- ○ proudly
- ○ speedily

4 **How were Rabbit and Turtle *alike* before the races?**

____

____

____

____

5 **Describe the changes in Turtle's feelings about himself from the beginning to the end of the story.**

____

____

____

____

____

____

Name ______________________________

Read the selection. Then answer the questions that follow.

The Foods We Eat

We have so many different kinds of food now! In one day, you might eat an apple, a tomato, and some bread. All these foods are easy to find today. Yet people did not always plant or prepare them.

People started growing apples around 10,000 years ago. We started planting tomatoes only about 3,000 years ago.

How do we know this? Scientists find bits and pieces of old foods around ancient fire places. Old paintings also show what people were eating once. People wrote about what they ate too.

The next time you eat an apple, think of a person long ago doing the same thing!

Timeline of Food

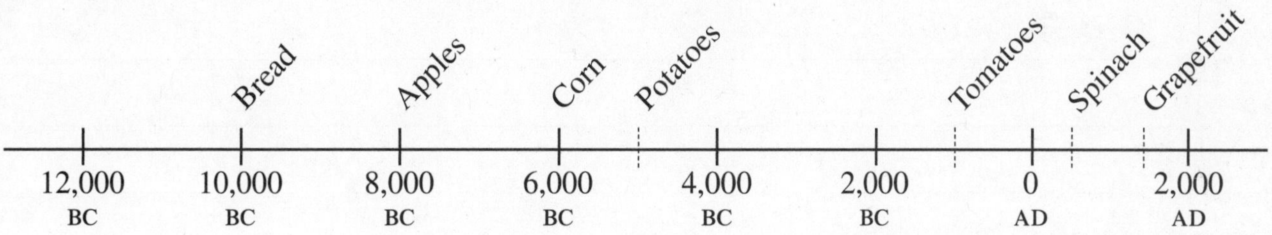

Turn the page.

Answer the questions below.

1 **According to the timeline, which of these foods did people start growing *first*?**

○ grapefruit
○ potatoes
○ corn
○ spinach

2 **According to the timeline, which of these was the *last* food that people began to grow?**

○ grapefruit
○ spinach
○ apples
○ tomatoes

3 **Why did the author write this selection?**

○ to tell a story about a person who likes to eat
○ to persuade the reader to grow different foods
○ to share information about food history
○ to explain which foods people are eating today

4 **What is one conclusion you can draw from the timeline?**

Name ___________________________________

Read the selection. Then answer the questions that follow.

The Picnic

Mr. Swenson's chess club was planning the annual club picnic, which was always open to every student from the school. The picnic would occur in the early summer after the end of the school year. The club members were considering which town park they should choose for their picnic.

"The park has to have picnic tables, so we can eat lunch," Mr. Swenson said.

"We need a playing field, too, so we can play baseball," said Jim.

"What about chess tables? Aren't we going to play chess? We are the chess club, after all," said Maria, laughing.

"What about a playground for the kids who don't want to play sports or chess?" asked Jim.

"And what if it rains?" asked Ming. "We need a park with a shelter so it won't rain on our parade . . . I mean, picnic."

"You people are thinking of all the features of the perfect place. That's great!" said Mr. Swenson. "Now let's examine this chart of the four town parks to check which one would be best."

CHESTER TOWN PARKS				
FEATURE	**River Park**	**Rainbow Park**	**Duck Park**	**Smith Park**
Playground	x	x	x	x
Ball Field	x	x	x	x
Picnic Tables	x		x	x
Shelter	x	x	x	
School Groups OK		x	x	x
Parking	x	x	x	x

"I'll call the Parks Office and ask whether Duck Park has chess tables. If not, we can bring our own boards," said Mr. Swenson.

"This is going to be the best picnic ever!" the club members cheered.

Turn the page.

Answer the questions below.

1 **What is the purpose of this selection?**

- ◯ to encourage you to join a club
- ◯ to explain how to pick the right park
- ◯ to persuade you to have a picnic
- ◯ to give an opinion about a park

2 **Based on the selection, which feature needs to be added to the chart?**

- ◯ Chess Tables
- ◯ Water Fountains
- ◯ Swimming Pool
- ◯ Sand Box

3 **The club will probably reject Smith Park because that park does *not* have**

- ◯ a picnic table.
- ◯ a ball field.
- ◯ a playground.
- ◯ a shelter.

4 **River Park *cannot* be used for the club picnic because it does *not***

- ◯ have a playground.
- ◯ allow school groups.
- ◯ have picnic tables.
- ◯ offer any parking.

5 **Based on the chart, which park do you think the club should choose for the picnic? Explain your answer.**

___

___

___

___

___

___

___

Name ______________________________________

Read the selection. Then answer the questions that follow.

Now You See Them, Now You Don't

Did you ever wish you could disappear? Some animals can hide, change their color, or look like something else so well that it looks as if they have disappeared. How an animal "disappears" depends on what it is and where it lives. A deer can't disappear in the same way a fish can.

Most animals hide to protect themselves from other animals, and a good way for an animal to hide is to match its looks to its environment. When a deer lies on the ground, it almost disappears because the deer is brown just like the ground. A squirrel climbs a tree when it wants to disappear because its fur is brown and rough like the tree bark.

Some animals change color when the season changes. In winter, Arctic foxes are white, but in summer, their fur turns dark to match the bare ground.

Other animals use their bodies or designs on their bodies to help them blend into their natural surroundings. When some creatures are hungry, they might overlook the insect called a walking stick because it looks like a tiny branch on a tree. Some fish that live in tall grass underwater have fins that look like swaying grass. When other fish swim by, they see only tall grass.

The next time you think there are no animals around, remember to look for those that might have disappeared.

How Animals Hide from Enemies	
Color	**Body Shape**
Deer—brown like the ground Squirrels—brown and blotchy like tree bark Arctic Fox— white like snow in winter	Walking Stick—looks like a little tree branch

Turn the page.

Answer the questions below.

1 **All the animals on the left side of the chart**

- ◯ are the same color as the trees.
- ◯ have hides with the same color fur.
- ◯ are the same color as where they live.
- ◯ change colors in different seasons.

2 **What is another good title for the chart?**

- ◯ "Animal Environments"
- ◯ "Three Ways That Animals Can Disappear"
- ◯ "What Animals Look Like"
- ◯ "How Animals Match Their Surroundings"

3 **Why did the author write this selection?**

- ◯ to tell a story about animals and where they live
- ◯ to explain how animals protect themselves
- ◯ to describe how people can learn from animals
- ◯ to express feelings about the way animals live

4 **What is the purpose of the chart?**

____

____

____

____

____

5 **State two facts from the selection that you could add to the chart. Tell where they belong on the chart.**

____

____

____

____

____

Name ____

Read the selection. Then answer the questions that follow.

Clever Foxes

Foxes are clever animals. They can feel at home either in the city or on a farm. Some animals cannot live where people live, but foxes do not mind if people live near them.

Foxes do not need to hunt for just the right kind of food. Foxes have been seen eating pizza! If they are not hungry, foxes will hide food. They dig a hole and put the food in the hole to eat later.

Foxes hunt at night. A good time to see them is when the sun is just coming up or going down. The next time you want to watch a beautiful and clever animal, keep your eyes open for a fox.

Turn the page.

Answer the questions below.

1 **What is true of all foxes?**

- ◯ They will eat almost anything.
- ◯ They hunt in the daytime.
- ◯ They live only in the country.
- ◯ They do not live where people live.

2 **What does this selection tell you about how foxes hunt?**

- ◯ They look for holes to hide in.
- ◯ They like to eat chickens.
- ◯ They hunt at night.
- ◯ They hunt for food during the day.

3 **In what way are foxes like squirrels?**

- ◯ Both live mostly in city parks.
- ◯ Both eat other small animals.
- ◯ Both are afraid to live near humans.
- ◯ Both will hide food to eat later.

4 **Give one reason you think foxes are clever animals.**

Name ___________________________________

Read the selection. Then answer the questions that follow.

Quack, Quack

Ducks are birds that are suited for the water. They have feet that look like paddles. These make ducks very good swimmers. Their feet have a specialized blood supply to keep them warm. Also, ducks have feathers that do not get wet because of a special oil that keeps their feathers dry.

The shape of a duck's bill, or mouth, tells how the duck gets its food. Some ducks have broad bills that help them sift the mud for insects and snails. Other ducks have long, narrow bills with sharp edges inside. These ducks catch and eat fish. If a duck's bill is wide and short, it eats plants and insects that it finds on or under the water.

Ducks are not only beautiful but also useful to people. Some give us eggs and meat, while others give us feathers for pillows and blankets. The feathers make the pillows soft and the blankets warm.

There are hundreds of types of ducks living in ponds, rivers, oceans, and marshes all over the world. The next time you see a duck, look at its bill to notice how and what it eats.

Turn the page.

Answer the questions below.

1 **What is one thing you can say about all ducks?**
- ○ They have broad bills.
- ○ They can swim.
- ○ They eat insects.
- ○ They eat plants.

2 **What is true of all ducks that have long, narrow bills with sharp edges?**
- ○ They live only in rivers.
- ○ They have clawed feet.
- ○ They catch and eat fish.
- ○ They go south for the winter.

3 **What does this selection tell you about where ducks live?**
- ○ They can live in either cold or warm water.
- ○ They get most of their food by living in marshes.
- ○ They have to get out of the water to stay warm.
- ○ They would rather be on the ground than in the water.

4 **In what way are ducks like other birds?**
- ○ Both have sharp teeth and beaks.
- ○ Both live in dens and on nests.
- ○ Both eat only fish and insects.
- ○ Both have feathers and can fly.

5 **How are ducks useful to people?**

Name ___________________________________

Read the selection. Then answer the questions that follow.

The Cold Really Is Common

Every person you know has probably had a cold, even you. Colds are one of the most common reasons people see their doctors. Colds are also a main reason people miss work and school.

Children in school get about six to ten colds every year. If there are many children in one family, they can get as many as twelve colds every year. Doctors believe that children in school get more colds because they work together in one room, so germs spread easily.

Some people once thought that you could catch a cold if the weather outside was cold, but this is not true. We know that one way to catch a cold is to touch something that has cold germs on it and then touch your eyes or nose. You can also get a cold if someone with a cold sneezes and you breathe in the germs.

One thing you can do to stay healthy is to wash your hands often. This will kill any germs that might be on your hands. You can help keep other people healthy by covering your mouth when you sneeze or cough.

There is no cure for the common cold, but many people are working hard to find one. Every person you know probably hopes someone will find a cure soon.

Turn the page.

Answer the questions below.

1 **After reading this selection, what can you say about most people and colds?**

- ◯ They work hard to find a cure for the cold.
- ◯ They cover their mouths when they cough.
- ◯ They wash their hands often.
- ◯ They have had a cold.

2 **Which clue word in paragraph one helps you make a generalization about people and colds?**

- ◯ every
- ◯ person
- ◯ hopes
- ◯ someone

3 **What is most likely true of children who have many colds every year?**

- ◯ They live where the weather changes a lot.
- ◯ They do not go to the doctor often enough.
- ◯ They live and work with other children who have colds.
- ◯ Their parents don't dress them warmly enough.

4 **What is one thing you can say about all people who catch colds?**

____

____

____

____

____

5 **What can you say about all people who cover their mouths when they sneeze?**

____

____

____

____

____

Name ___________________________________

Read the selection. Then answer the questions that follow.

Crash!

Vic was excited about his new toy, a race car from the movie "Race Boys." When Vic saw the movie, he wanted that car very much. Dad said Vic could buy it with his own money. So Vic worked around the house and earned enough money.

Vic raced it across the living room floor with his other cars. Then he pushed it really hard toward the kitchen. It crashed into the corner! A wheel fell off!

Dad said, "Toys seem to break easily now. They are not made well anymore." Maybe Dad was right. Vic hoped Dad could fix it. He could usually fix almost anything.

Turn the page.

Answer the questions below.

1 **What does Dad think is true about most new toys?**

- ◯ They cannot be fixed.
- ◯ They cost too much money.
- ◯ They do not last long.
- ◯ They are strong and sturdy.

2 **Why did Vic do work around the house?**

- ◯ He wanted to show Dad that he was a good son.
- ◯ He wanted to play on a clean living room floor.
- ◯ He wanted to make money to pay for a new toy.
- ◯ He wanted to thank Dad for fixing his new car.

3 **How did Vic get his idea to buy a toy race car?**

- ◯ His old race car had gotten broken.
- ◯ His Dad suggested he get a race car.
- ◯ He did not have any other race cars.
- ◯ He saw the race car in a movie.

4 **What caused Vic's toy to break?**

Name ____

Read the selection. Then answer the questions that follow.

Bees and Wasps

You probably know that both bees and wasps can sting, but what else do you know about them? Did you know that after a honeybee stings you, the bee dies? This happens because the stinger gets stuck in you. Pulling it out means the bee would lose part of its body. A wasp and other types of bees can pull out their stingers and sting someone else—or sting you again.

Did you know that both bees and wasps can make nests? Bees' nests are called hives, and bees use them to store their food as well as to take care of baby bees. Wasps use their nests only for taking care of baby wasps.

How many insects can make their own food? Bees collect pollen and turn it into honey, which bees eat. Bees can also communicate with each other. They communicate by dancing, or moving their wings and bodies in special ways. When one bee finds a good place to collect pollen, it will fly back to the nest and dance to tell the other bees.

Wasps eat other insects. They may also drink nectar from flowers.

If a bee or a wasp comes buzzing around your head, just stand still and give it a chance to fly away. It is probably just curious about you.

Turn the page.

Answer the questions below.

1 Why does a bee die after it stings somebody?

- ◯ When a bee stings people, it has to drink its own poison.
- ◯ The stinger stays stuck in people, and the bee cannot live without it.
- ◯ People usually hit the bee, and that almost always kills it.
- ◯ The bee gets poisoned by the oils that are in everybody's skin.

2 Why do bees collect pollen?

- ◯ They need it to feed the other insects.
- ◯ They can use it to decorate their nests.
- ◯ They make it into honey that they eat.
- ◯ They can find a good place to store it.

3 Why do bees dance?

- ◯ to have a good time
- ◯ to get some exercise
- ◯ to warm up in the cold
- ◯ to share information

4 What is one reason bees or wasps probably come near you?

- ◯ They like to walk on your skin.
- ◯ They want to find out about you.
- ◯ They like to drink your sweat.
- ◯ They want to lead you to their nests.

5 Based on this selection, what is a general statement that can be made about all bees and wasps?

Name ____________________________________

Read the selection. Then answer the questions that follow.

Nancy and Lisa

A long time ago there were two mice, a city mouse and a country mouse. One day the city mouse, Nancy, came to visit the country mouse, Lisa. Nancy looked around Lisa's cozy hole on the side of the hill. Nancy said that it was not very big and that the tables and chairs had scratches and looked old. Lisa just smiled and told Nancy that the furniture had belonged to her mother and that it reminded her of her mom.

"I prefer new things," said Nancy.

"Let's have a snack," Lisa said, and she put some nuts and corn on the old table. They sat down on the comfortable chairs and ate peacefully.

The next week, Lisa went to visit Nancy in the city. When she got to Nancy's hole in the wall, Nancy told her to sneak in quickly because of the cat. Lisa had never seen a cat before. Suddenly a huge creature jumped at her, but luckily Lisa was close enough to the hole to escape danger. Lisa still felt nervous when they sat down in Nancy's fancy new chairs at her fancy new table. Nancy put cheese and fruit on the table, but the cat kept clawing at the hole, making so much noise that Lisa could not eat. Nancy could.

When Lisa got home, all she said was, "It's good to be home again."

Turn the page.

Answer the questions below.

1 **What probably caused Lisa's furniture to get scratched?**

- ◯ being clawed by the cat
- ◯ being used for a long time
- ◯ being hurt in an accident
- ◯ being damaged by nut shells

2 **What happened that made Lisa sneak quickly into Nancy's home?**

- ◯ The cat blocked off the hole.
- ◯ The cat jumped at her.
- ◯ The cat made a lot of noise.
- ◯ The cat went away.

3 **Why was Lisa *not* able to eat at Nancy's home?**

- ◯ She did not eat cheese and fruit.
- ◯ She already ate lunch at home.
- ◯ She did not like the fancy table.
- ◯ She was afraid of the huge cat.

4 **Why did Lisa say, "It's good to be home again," at the end of the story?**

____

____

____

____

____

____

5 **Write a general statement that describes something this story teaches you about people.**

____

____

____

____

____

Name ______________________________________

Read the selection. Then answer the questions that follow.

Boats

People have been making boats for over 6,000 years. All boats can float on water. Boats have been made of many things. Some boats were made of reeds. Some were made of tree trunks. Today, most boats are fiberglass or aluminum. A few are still made of wood. Big ships are made of steel.

Boats can be moved in different ways. If the water is not deep, people can use poles to push. In deep water, people can paddle. About 4,000 years ago the Egyptians discovered the wind could move boats. The first sail boat had a square cotton sail. Today, engines move motor boats and ships. But people still use sail boats for fun.

Turn the page.

Answer the questions below.

1 **In what way are all boats *alike*?**

- ◯ All boats have cotton sails.
- ◯ All boats float on water.
- ◯ All boats are made of reeds.
- ◯ All boats have engines.

2 **How are all sail boats the *same*?**

- ◯ They all use wind to move.
- ◯ They all are made from wood.
- ◯ They all use paddles to move.
- ◯ They all are made in Egypt.

3 **What does the picture show?**

- ◯ why a boat can float
- ◯ how boats are made
- ◯ different kinds of boats
- ◯ all boats that use engines

4 **According to the selection, how are most boats built today?**

Name ____________________________________

Read the selection. Then answer the questions that follow.

Your Lungs

Your lungs work hard breathing every minute of every day. Lungs are some of the largest organs in your body. Your lungs fill up almost your whole chest. Everyone has two lungs. The lung on the left side is a little smaller. This leaves room on that side for your heart to fit in.

If you could see your lungs, they would look pink and something like a sponge. Two large tubes connect the lungs to your windpipe. Your windpipe connects to your mouth.

Under your lungs is your diaphragm, a large, dome-shaped muscle. When you breathe in, your diaphragm flattens out so your lungs can fill with air. When you breathe out, your diaphragm moves up to push air out of your lungs.

Adults breathe about ten to twenty times each minute when they are just relaxing. Children breathe faster, about twenty to thirty times each minute. When you exercise, your breathing rate increases.

Oxygen from the air you breathe passes through your lungs into your blood.

Smoking damages your lungs. They get clogged with dirt and cannot work correctly. Exercise helps make your lungs stronger. So, do not smoke, but do exercise to keep your lungs healthy!

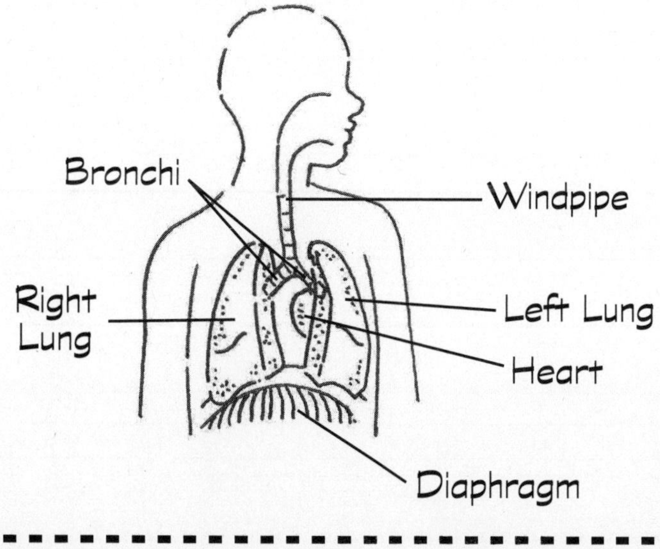

Turn the page.

Answer the questions below.

1 **What is generally true about how to keep your lungs healthy?**

- ◯ Exercise will make your lungs wear out sooner.
- ◯ If your diaphragm moves up, you will breathe air in.
- ◯ Lungs should relax at night after working hard all day.
- ◯ If you smoke, your lungs will stop working properly.

2 **Based on the diagram, what is the name for the two tubes that connect the lungs to the windpipe?**

- ◯ diaphragm
- ◯ bronchi
- ◯ heart
- ◯ head

3 **How are everyone's lungs alike?**

- ◯ They get clogged with dirt.
- ◯ They make you stronger.
- ◯ They help people breathe.
- ◯ They make oxygen for you.

4 **Which of these is usually true about the way people breathe?**

- ◯ People breathe in oxygen using only their left lung.
- ◯ Adults often breathe more than thirty times each minute.
- ◯ People breathe faster when they exercise hard.
- ◯ Children breathe much more slowly than adults do.

5 **Based on this selection, what can you say about the way most lungs look?**

Name ___________________________________

Read the selection. Then answer the questions that follow.

Tree Rings

If you studied a tree stump, you would notice a pattern of circles radiating from its center to its outside edge. These circles, or rings, show the age of the tree. A tree produces new wood around its trunk every year. Usually, one layer of wood grows annually. Each layer has two colors of wood: a light-colored layer that grows in spring and summer and a darker, denser layer that grows in autumn and winter. When you count up all the layers, you can determine how old the tree is.

You do not have to cut down a tree to study its rings. A narrow metal tube can be drilled into its trunk from its outside edge to its center. This way you remove a slender core of wood and get a sample to analyze. This does not injure trees. It can be done with living trees or dead ones.

Tree rings do not tell just the tree's age. They also provide a glimpse into what the weather was like each year. Tree rings grow thin in dry years and thick in wet years. In California, where the weather is dry and preserves wood, scientists have studied ancient wood found at archaeological sites. The weather information collected from these tree rings dates back 8,000 years.

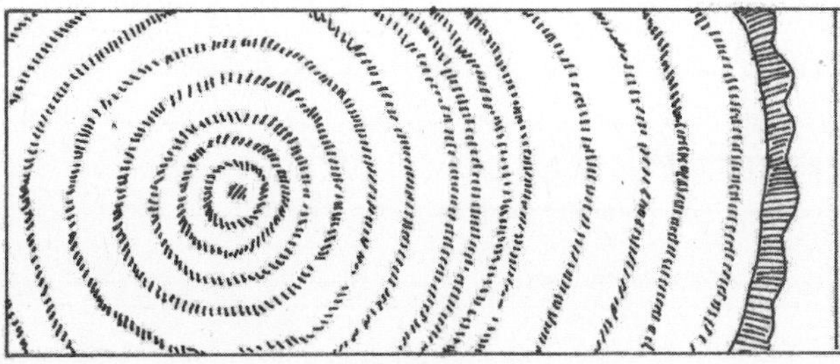

Figure A

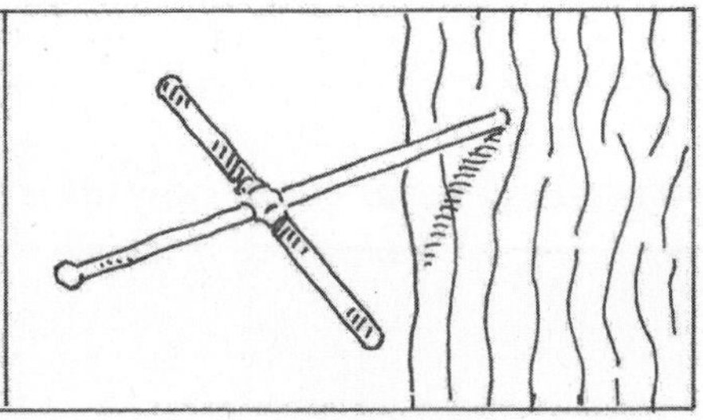

Figure B

Turn the page.

Answer the questions below.

1 **One way that all tree rings are *alike* is that**

- ◯ The oldest rings are exact circles.
- ◯ The rings are a way to figure out the age of a tree.
- ◯ The rings stack up from the ground to the tree's top.
- ◯ The thickest rings are the same size in wet years.

2 **According to the selection, which of the following statements is true of all tree rings?**

- ◯ They are created from ancient wood.
- ◯ They can provide a current weather report.
- ◯ They are dense but light-colored.
- ◯ They can show the growth of a tree.

3 **The picture labeled B shows**

- ◯ how a person counts up light and dark tree rings.
- ◯ what the weather must have been like years ago.
- ◯ how a person collects a core sample from a tree.
- ◯ what tree rings would look like on an older tree.

4 **Based upon the information in the selection, why do scientists usually study tree rings?**

____

____

____

____

____

____

5 **What can you say in general about how all trees grow thicker?**

____

____

____

____

____

Name ________________________________

Read the selection. Then answer the questions that follow.

Something Fishy

When you think of fish in the ocean, do you think of dolphins? Dolphins live in the ocean, but they are not fish.

Both fish and dolphins need air to live, but they breathe differently. Fish do not have lungs. They have gills. They take in air from the water when water passes over their gills.

Dolphins have lungs like humans, so they must come to the surface of the water to get air. They have small holes on the top of their heads where the air comes in and out.

Fish and dolphins do not even swim the same way. Fish move their tails from side to side, but dolphins move their tails up and down.

Fish and dolphins are different, but both are fun to watch.

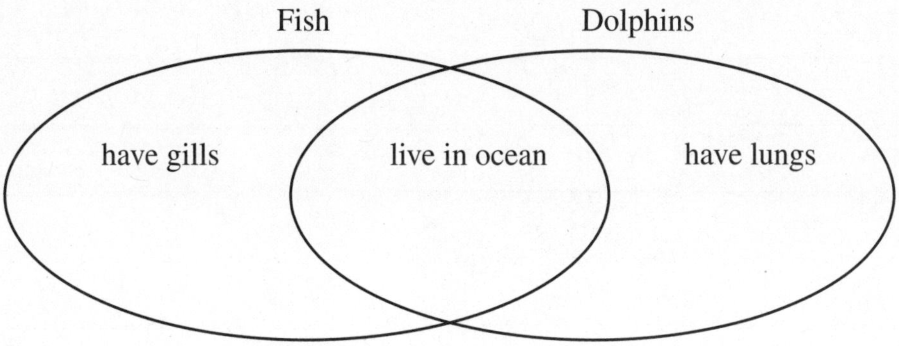

Turn the page.

Answer the questions below.

1 **In the diagram, which detail could be added to the Fish circle?**

- ○ need lungs to breathe air
- ○ need to come to the surface
- ○ take in air from the water
- ○ have holes on top of head

2 **In the diagram, which one could be added to the Dolphins circle?**

- ○ can breathe air underwater
- ○ move tails up and down
- ○ do not need lungs to breathe
- ○ move tails from side to side

3 **Which of these states the main idea of the *fourth* paragraph?**

- ○ When people think of fish, they think of dolphins.
- ○ Dolphins push their tails up and down to move.
- ○ Fish and dolphins are different in how they swim.
- ○ Fish always move their tails from side to side.

4 **In the diagram, what else could be put in the center section where the circles overlap?**

Name ____________________________________

Read the selection. Then answer the questions that follow.

Table Manners

People in different countries have their own ways of doing things. Even the way people eat changes. People in China do not have the same customs as people in America.

In China, people use chopsticks to eat. Chopsticks are a pair of long, thin, wooden sticks that take the place of a fork. There is a special way to hold them, using the fingers of one hand. But they do not use chopsticks for everything. They use spoons to eat soup, just as in America.

In America, when you finish eating, you should place your knife and fork on top of your plate. In China it is very important to lay the chopsticks across the top of the rice bowl, which also shows that you have finished eating. If you place the chopsticks straight up in a bowl of rice, people will think you wish them bad luck. This is because when someone dies in China, it is a custom to place two sticks of incense upright in a bowl of rice or sand on a shrine.

In China, there is also a proper way to place a teapot on the table. The spout should not point toward anyone, but toward a place where nobody is sitting.

Whether you use chopsticks or forks, it is always polite to thank the cook after you eat.

China	America	Both Countries
use chopsticks	use knives and forks	use spoons

Turn the page.

Answer the questions below.

1 **In the chart, which of these could be added in the column under the heading "China"?**

- ◯ lay chopsticks across top of bowl
- ◯ put chopsticks straight up in bowl
- ◯ place bowls of sand on dinner tables
- ◯ hold forks in the right hand only

2 **In the chart, what could be added in the column under the heading "America"?**

- ◯ be polite and thank the cook when meal is over
- ◯ place knife and fork on top of plate after finishing
- ◯ place bowls of rice or sand with incense on shrines
- ◯ use just one wooden chopstick when you eat

3 **In the chart, which of these should be added under the heading "Both Countries"?**

- ◯ point your fork where nobody is sitting
- ◯ never use knives for cutting food
- ◯ always have a teapot on the table
- ◯ thank the person who cooked the meal

4 **What is the main idea of the *second* paragraph?**

- ◯ In China, people use only chopsticks for eating every kind of food.
- ◯ People in China use chopsticks to eat instead of using forks.
- ◯ You must hold your chopsticks carefully in the fingers of one hand.
- ◯ Table manners and polite customs are different in every country.

5 **Why would it be best to put "use bowls" in the last column on the chart?**

Name ____

Read the selection. Then answer the questions that follow.

Biomes

A biome is an area of the world where the environment determines the type of plants and animals that live there. Deserts and tropical rain forests are biomes that you probably know about. However, you may not know about tundra and taiga, which are biomes in the northern part of the world.

Tundra is the coldest and driest biome on Earth. There are no trees and not many plants because the ground is always frozen. Because tundra is located far north, the position of the sun creates nights that may last as long as two months in the winter and a day in summer that may last almost twenty-four hours. Animals such as deer, rabbits, and wolves can live in the tundra biome. Some birds live there in the summer, and some fish can live in the cold water.

Taiga is south of the tundra biome, so it is not as cold. There are few plants in taiga, but evergreens can grow tall because they have a covering on their needles that protects them from the cold. Taiga is home to many of the same kinds of animals and birds that live in the tundra biome. In the summer, millions of insects live on tundra and taiga. They provide food for birds.

Tundra and taiga are home to some plants and animals that can't live anywhere else, which makes these biomes valuable to our planet.

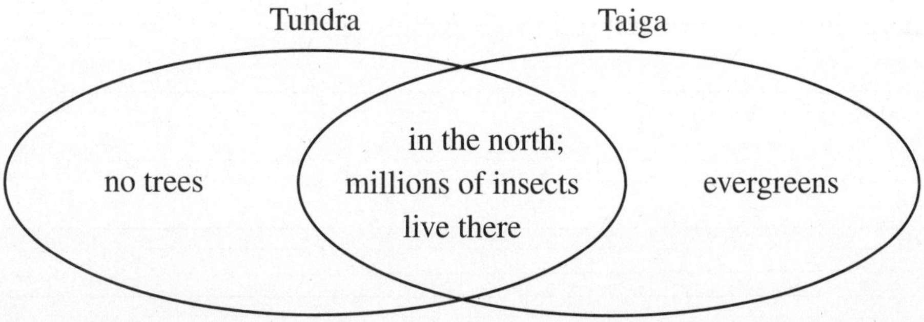

Turn the page.

Answer the questions below.

1 In the diagram, which of the following does not belong in the Tundra circle?

- ◯ driest biome on Earth
- ◯ birds live there all year
- ◯ ground always frozen
- ◯ animals cannot live there

2 In the diagram, which one of the following could be added to the center section?

- ◯ far south
- ◯ hot summers
- ◯ rain forest
- ◯ some plants

3 What is the main idea of the *second* paragraph?

- ◯ The northern biomes are home to animals that do not live anywhere else.
- ◯ The cold and dryness limit the plants and animals that live in the tundra.
- ◯ The birds come to live in the tundra biome during the summer months.
- ◯ The plants that grow in tundra have to be able to live in frozen ground.

4 What things about the tundra biome and the taiga biome are shown in the center section of the Venn diagram?

____

____

____

____

____

____

5 How does the diagram help the reader understand this selection?

____

____

____

____

Name ______________________________

Read the selection. Then answer the questions that follow.

Yo-Yo Ma

Yo-Yo Ma is an amazing musician. People love to listen to his music.

Ma was born in Paris in 1955. Later, his family moved to New York. His parents are Chinese. His mother was a great singer. His father was a great musician too. At first, Ma played the violin. He did not like it that much, so he played the cello instead.

Ma performed for the first time when he was just five years old. He played on television when he was eight. He was a young wonder.

Today, Yo-Yo Ma plays all different kinds of music for cello. His music is always interesting.

Turn the page.

Answer the questions below.

1 **What caused Yo-Yo Ma to stop playing the violin?**

- ◯ He learned that he was not good at it.
- ◯ He found out that he did not like it.
- ◯ He performed on radio and television.
- ◯ He moved from Paris to New York.

2 **Which sentence from the selection is a statement of opinion?**

- ◯ Yo-Yo Ma is an amazing musician.
- ◯ Yo-Yo Ma was born in Paris in 1955.
- ◯ Later, his family moved to New York.
- ◯ His parents are Chinese.

3 **Which sentence from the selection is a statement of fact?**

- ◯ His mother was a great singer.
- ◯ His father was a great musician too.
- ◯ He played on television when he was eight.
- ◯ He was a young wonder.

4 **The last sentence in the selection is a statement of opinion. How can you tell it is?**

Name ______________________________

Read the selection. Then answer the questions that follow.

The First Lady of Song

Ella Fitzgerald was "the best there ever was. Amongst all of us who sing, she was the best." The great singer Johnny Mathis said those words, and most people would agree with him. Ella Fitzgerald was an amazing performer of jazz and popular song. She has inspired many other singers.

Fitzgerald was born in Virginia but later moved to New York. At first, Fitzgerald's dream was to dance. At sixteen, she entered a contest at the Apollo Theater. But when she walked onto the stage, she froze. Instead of dancing, she sang a song. The crowd loved it. Fitzgerald took first prize in the contest.

After she finished school, Fitzgerald joined the Chick Webb Band. She became a star with a lot of hit songs.

From the 1950s through the 1970s, Fitzgerald continued to impress audiences with her singing. She performed with all the best jazz musicians of her time. She was a true genius at performing. She was the best performer at "scat" singing. This is when a singer uses nonsense syllables to make the sounds of musical instruments.

Fitzgerald performed for fifty-eight years. In that time, she won thirteen Grammy awards and sold more than forty million records. She has surely been the First Lady of Song.

Turn the page.

Answer the questions below.

1 **Which of these is a statement of fact?**

- ◯ Fitzgerald was the best singer ever.
- ◯ Fitzgerald was born in Virginia.
- ◯ She was the best at "scat" singing.
- ◯ She must be the First Lady of Song.

2 **Which of these is a statement of opinion?**

- ◯ She later moved to New York.
- ◯ She sold more than forty million records.
- ◯ She was an amazing jazz performer.
- ◯ She performed for fifty-eight years.

3 **What happened that caused Ella Fitzgerald to sing a song at the Apollo Theater?**

- ◯ She joined the Chick Webb Band.
- ◯ She became too afraid to dance.
- ◯ She became a famous performer.
- ◯ She moved from Virginia to New York.

4 **Write a statement of fact about Ella Fitzgerald. Explain why it is a fact.**

____

____

____

____

____

5 **Read the following sentence from the selection: She was a true genius at performing. Explain how you can tell that the sentence is a statement of opinion.**

____

____

____

____

____

Name ______________________________

Read the selection. Then answer the questions that follow.

Wynton Marsalis

Wynton Marsalis is probably the best trumpet player who ever lived. He is not only a famous musician, but he is a great man as well. He has helped many young people learn to appreciate and play jazz and classical music.

Wynton was born in New Orleans in 1961 into a musical family. He showed his talent early. At age eight, he played in a church band, and at fourteen, he performed with the New Orleans Philharmonic. At nineteen, after some time in college, Marsalis joined the famous Jazz Messengers. This was one of the best jazz bands around. Marsalis learned a lot and soon formed his own band, which he took on tour around the world.

Not satisfied just to be the best in jazz, when he was twenty, Marsalis started performing classical music too. And he started composing his own music.

Marsalis also became an educator. He wrote an excellent series of television and radio shows about music. He also established a jazz concert series that exposes more people to that art form.

In his life, Marsalis has made more than sixty records and won many, many awards. He continues to perform, write new music, and help others learn and grow. He is truly a gifted, energetic, and inspiring man.

Turn the page.

Answer the questions below.

1 **Which sentence from the selection is a statement of opinion?**

- ○ He is not only a famous musician, but he is a great man as well.
- ○ He has helped many young people learn to appreciate and play jazz and classical music.
- ○ He also established a jazz concert series that exposes more people to that art form.
- ○ He continues to perform, write new music, and help others learn and grow.

2 **Which sentence from the selection is a statement of fact?**

- ○ Wynton Marsalis is probably the best trumpet player who ever lived.
- ○ At age eight, he played in a church band, and at fourteen, he performed with the New Orleans Philharmonic.
- ○ This was one of the best jazz bands around.
- ○ He wrote an excellent series of television and radio shows about music.

3 **The last sentence in the selection is a statement of opinion. How do you know?**

- ○ It gives factual information about Wynton Marsalis.
- ○ It shows the author's feelings about Wynton Marsalis.
- ○ It makes a general statement about Wynton Marsalis.
- ○ It compares Wynton Marsalis with other musicians.

4 **Based upon the selection, what effect might Wynton Marsalis's family have had on his career?**

____

____

____

____

____

5 **Write a statement of fact from the selection. Explain why this is a statement of fact.**

____

____

____

____

____

Name ______________________________________

Read the selection. Then answer the questions that follow.

Bicycle Safety

Riding a bicycle is the best way to have fun, but you should always wear something to protect your head. Many states have laws about bicycle safety. Your state may require you to wear a helmet when you ride. You should learn about the safety laws in your state.

The best kind of helmet should sit straight on your head and make contact with your head at all times. If you can move the helmet after you buckle the strap, it is not a good fit. Helmets do not cost a lot of money. They come in many colors, but red helmets look the best.

Most helmets are padded and have a thin plastic cover. The plastic will make the helmet slide on the hard ground if you should fall. This protects your head and neck.

No matter when or where you ride a bicycle, be safe and wear a helmet.

Turn the page.

Answer the questions below.

1 **The first sentence in the selection is a statement of opinion. How do you know?**

- ◯ because the first sentence is usually an opinion
- ◯ because it tells how only one person feels about riding bicycles
- ◯ because a person did not say it
- ◯ because bicycles are not made just for fun

2 **Which sentence from the selection is a statement of fact?**

- ◯ Many states have laws about bicycle safety.
- ◯ Red helmets look the best.
- ◯ Helmets do not cost a lot of money.
- ◯ Be safe and wear a helmet.

3 **What is true of most bicycle helmets?**

- ◯ The best helmets are red.
- ◯ All bicycle riders wear them.
- ◯ The outside of the helmet is plastic.
- ◯ They should not touch the head.

4 **Write a statement of fact from the third paragraph.**

Name ________________________________

Read the selection. Then answer the questions that follow.

Settlers' Lights

Today, people can buy candles with different shapes, colors, sizes, and even smells, although we no longer need to use candles as a main source of light. Years ago, settlers worked hard to light their cabins, and they did not worry about how candles looked or smelled. Making candles was a dirty job that took hours, so people were happy to have any kind of candle.

Many years ago, people made candles from the fat of the animals they killed for food. They melted the fat, boiled it in water, strained it, and then cooled it. Some people added spices to the hot fat so that it would not smell bad.

Dipping was an easy way to make candles. String was dipped into the hot fat, taken out, and then cooled. The string was dipped and cooled many times, each time adding another layer of fat, until the candle was the desired size. Even children enjoyed dipping candles.

Some settlers used molds that looked like tall metal boxes with holes at the top. Strings were put into the holes, and hot fat was poured in. The candles were cooled and then taken out. Molds were not as messy as dipping, and one person could make many candles at once.

Making candles was hard work, but having light was worth the effort.

Turn the page.

Answer the questions below.

1 **Which sentence is a statement of fact?**

- ○ People made candles from the fat of animals.
- ○ Dipping was an easy way to make candles.
- ○ Children were good at dipping candles.
- ○ Making candles was hard work.

2 **Which sentence is a statement of opinion?**

- ○ Some people added spices to the hot fat.
- ○ Some settlers used molds that looked like tall metal boxes.
- ○ Molds were not as messy as dipping.
- ○ One person could make many candles at once.

3 **What do you think most candles the settlers made looked like?**

- ○ They were different sizes and shapes.
- ○ They were shaped like animals.
- ○ They were small because the cabins were small.
- ○ They were short and fat.

4 **How might the author know what candle molds looked like?**

- ○ by seeing them in a museum
- ○ by buying them at a store
- ○ by visiting a modern candle factory
- ○ by looking at candles made today

5 **How could you find out whether this selection contains facts?**

____

____

____

____

____

____

____

____

Name ____

Read the selection. Then answer the questions that follow.

American Hero

Cesar Chavez (1927–1993) became one of the most famous people in America by organizing migrant farm workers. These are workers who travel from farm to farm looking for work as the seasons change and different crops need to be harvested. Chavez himself was a migrant worker, so he understood what it was like to be one. His life is one of the most fascinating stories in American history.

Most migrant workers lived in poor conditions. The children did not attend school because families were always moving to find work.

Chavez saw how unfairly the workers were being treated by the farm owners. The workers made very little money, worked long hours, and had no rights. Chavez talked about making changes.

He traveled from farm to farm teaching the workers how to read and write. He talked to them about how they could improve their lives. All the workers wanted to learn, but they were afraid they would lose their jobs if they made demands.

Chavez believed in nonviolent methods, such as marches and boycotts, to bring about change. He was very brave. By fasting, or not eating, for long periods of time, Chavez began to draw attention to the problems of migrant workers. People from around the country took notice. His strong leadership was admired and respected by all Americans.

Thanks to Cesar Chavez, the lives of many migrant farm workers have been greatly improved.

Turn the page.

Answer the questions below.

1 **Which sentence is a statement of fact?**

- ◯ Cesar Chavez became one of the most famous people in America.
- ◯ Migrant workers travel from farm to farm looking for work.
- ◯ His life is one of the most fascinating stories in American history.
- ◯ Cesar Chavez was a strong and able leader.

2 **Which sentence is a statement of opinion?**

- ◯ Chavez was a migrant worker.
- ◯ In 1945, most migrant workers did not own homes.
- ◯ Cesar Chavez was very brave.
- ◯ He traveled from farm to farm, teaching.

3 **Which of the following would be the best source of information about Cesar Chavez?**

- ◯ a book about American farms
- ◯ a biography of Cesar Chavez
- ◯ a picture of Cesar Chavez
- ◯ a movie about farm workers

4 **What is your opinion of Cesar Chavez? Write one sentence telling why you think as you do.**

5 **Write another statement of fact about migrant farm workers.**

Name ________________________________

Read the selection. Then answer the questions that follow.

Where Was Max?

Every day when Nina got home from school, her dog, Max, was waiting to say hello, but today when she walked into her house, Max wasn't there. *Where was Max?*

She went to her room, but Max was not under the bed.

Maybe Max was in the yard, she thought. Nina looked in the bushes and near the porch, but she could not find Max.

Nina was worried. She went back into the house and looked at the hook where Max's leash should have been, but it was not there. Could someone have taken him?

Just then Mom came into the house with Max on his leash. "I took Max to get the shots he needs to stay healthy," Mom said.

"I'm glad you're both home," said Nina, and Max barked in agreement.

Turn the page.

Answer the questions below.

1 **What causes Nina to be worried when she gets home?**

- ◯ She has walked there alone.
- ◯ Her dog has barked at her.
- ◯ She is unable to find her dog.
- ◯ She has to search the bushes.

2 **For what purpose did Mom take Max away with her?**

- ◯ Max needed to get some shots.
- ◯ Mom wanted to go walking with him.
- ◯ Max needed to get a new leash.
- ◯ Mom wanted to hide him from Nina.

3 **Why was Max's leash missing from the hook where it belonged?**

- ◯ Nina had lost the leash in the bushes.
- ◯ Mom had removed the leash to take Max.
- ◯ Nina had left the leash in her bedroom.
- ◯ Max had hidden the leash near the porch.

4 **What can you say is usually true of Max?**

Name ____________________________________

Read the selection. Then answer the questions that follow.

Addo's Poster

Addo's class was going to visit the science museum on Thursday. He knew he would want to buy the poster that showed Earth as seen by astronauts in space, but he didn't have enough money. He had already bought candy with all of his allowance money.

Addo picked up his glass Liberty Bell bank and thought about breaking it, but he saw that there were only a few nickels and dimes in it. That would not be enough for the poster.

Addo asked Mom for some money, but she reminded him about the family rule: Allowance is given every Friday. No exceptions.

Addo asked Mom what he could do to earn money before next Thursday.

"Mr. Linnet said he would pay you to feed and walk his dog," Mom said.

Addo made a deal with Mr. Linnet to walk and feed the dog every weekday. On Monday, Addo started his job. It was not a hard job, but afterward Addo had to walk home, eat dinner, and do his homework. He was very busy that week. In fact, he was so busy that he didn't have time to spend any money. When Mr. Linnet paid him, Addo was surprised to be paid so much money.

When Addo got home he told Mom how much money he'd earned.

"You also saved that much money from your allowance," she said, smiling.

"I can buy the poster now," he said proudly.

Turn the page.

Answer the questions below.

1 **What caused Addo's desire to earn more money?**

- ◯ He wanted to join the class trip.
- ◯ He wanted to buy a poster.
- ◯ He wanted to get some candy.
- ◯ He wanted to have his own dog.

2 **What did Addo learn in this story?**

- ◯ Working and going to school are tiring.
- ◯ If you break a rule, you will be sorry.
- ◯ If you work and save money, you can buy what you want.
- ◯ If you are busy, time goes by fast.

3 **Because Addo was taking care of Mr. Linnet's dog,**

- ◯ he was too busy to do his homework.
- ◯ he spent his money on dinners out.
- ◯ he was too busy to shop for candy.
- ◯ he stopped needing any allowance.

4 **For what reason did Mom refuse to give Addo money?**

- ◯ She had no time to go to the science museum.
- ◯ The family had already spent their whole budget.
- ◯ She did not like to take care of their neighbor's dog.
- ◯ The family had a rule against paying allowance early.

5 **Explain the reasons that led Addo to decide against breaking his glass Liberty Bell bank.**

Name ________________________________

Read the selection. Then answer the questions that follow.

Jack's Friend

Vance was a giant who lived alone in a gigantic castle. The townspeople who lived nearby feared and disliked anyone who was different. They especially disliked large people who could pick them up in one hand. So when Vance went to town, people stared at him. The stares hurt his feelings. He was a tender-hearted giant with sensitive feelings.

One day when Vance was out for a stroll, he nearly stumbled over a small gentleman who could only hear the giant's booming footsteps.

"You must be quite large!" said the gentleman as he turned toward the sound. "My name is Jack McGillicutty. What's yours?"

Vance was so shocked that all he could say was, "Aren't you afraid of me?"

But Jack wasn't afraid. He even asked Vance to help him find the post office, which Vance was happy to do.

"Thank you, and I hope we meet again soon," said Jack. Vance mentioned that he planned to go out walking again the next day, so they agreed to meet.

The next day, Vance leaned against a mountain while Jack sat on a bench at his feet. As they talked about music, some people came by and pointed at them. Vance stomped his feet, scaring all the finger-pointers away.

"What happened, my friend?" said Jack.

Vance was glad Jack could not see the tiny tear on his cheek.

"Oh, nothing," was all he could say.

Turn the page.

Answer the questions below.

1 **The townspeople disliked Vance because**

- ○ He lived alone in a gigantic castle.
- ○ He had become Jack's best friend.
- ○ He was clumsy and often stumbled.
- ○ He was different and very large.

2 **Why was Jack the only person unafraid of Vance?**

- ○ Jack had some rocks for protection.
- ○ Jack could not see he was a giant.
- ○ Jack knew about him from the others.
- ○ Jack did not know Vance liked music.

3 **What effect did Vance have when he stomped his feet?**

- ○ Jack laughed and began dancing.
- ○ The townspeople started weeping.
- ○ Jack wanted to find the post office.
- ○ The townspeople were scared away.

4 **For what reason was Vance crying at the end of the story?**

____

____

____

____

____

5 **What can you say about both Jack and Vance?**

____

____

____

____

____

____

Name ______________________________

Read the selection. Then answer the questions that follow.

Sparrows

The song sparrow and the house sparrow are birds that look almost alike, but you can tell them apart if you know what to look for. The song sparrow and the house sparrow can be found in almost every yard in North America. The next time you see a sparrow, look at its chest. The song sparrow has a white chest with dark lines below its neck, while the house sparrow's chest does not have any lines.

Then look at its neck. All song sparrows have a white neck with two stripes on each side. The male house sparrow has a black neck and white cheeks. The female house sparrow has a grayish white neck without any distinctive stripes.

Even their songs are not the same. A house sparrow sings "cheep, cheep." A song sparrow sings more varied notes.

The next time you see a sparrow in your yard, look at its chest and its neck. Then listen to its song. By keeping these descriptions in mind, you will be able to see and hear the difference.

Turn the page.

Answer the questions below.

1 **How are a song sparrow and a house sparrow alike?**

- ○ They both live in North America.
- ○ They both have white cheeks.
- ○ They both have lines on their chests.
- ○ They both have the same kind of song.

2 **How are a song sparrow and a house sparrow different?**

- ○ A song sparrow has a black neck, and a house sparrow has a white neck.
- ○ A song sparrow has a more varied song.
- ○ A house sparrow has more lines on its neck.
- ○ A house sparrow lives in a house, and a song sparrow lives in a yard.

3 **You are told to look at the sparrow's chest and neck because**

- ○ this is how to tell the two kinds apart.
- ○ it has a brown throat in North America.
- ○ this is the most colorful part of any bird.
- ○ it has a strong throat to sing its songs.

4 **How is the chest of a song sparrow different from that of a house sparrow?**

Name ___________________________________

Read the selection. Then answer the questions that follow.

Castles

You might think that castles exist only in fairy tales, but castles are real places that were used by real people long ago. Castles in Japan and in England did not look the same, but they were all built as forts to protect people and animals.

English castles were usually built using stone or bricks. Japanese castles were usually made of wood. In both countries castles had moats, or small rivers, around them to protect people and animals within the walls. The bridge across the moat could be pulled up to keep out unwanted people.

Both countries developed a style of castle with inner walls as well as an outer wall. This meant that an attacker who got past the outer wall would still not reach the people who lived inside.

In the center of a Japanese castle of this kind was a tower that could be well defended. The lords of the castle usually lived in another group of buildings. The warriors lived outside the castle, but nearby in case there was an attack.

In England, living in a castle was like living in a small town. Castles were always busy places with farmers, animals, and soldiers.

Today castles are not used in the same way that they were used many years ago. In each country we can visit castles and imagine how people once lived.

Turn the page.

Answer the questions below.

1 **In both England and Japan, how were the people who lived in castles alike?**

- ◯ They were warriors who defended the castle.
- ◯ They were farmers who kept cows and pigs.
- ◯ They were people who were protected by the castle walls.
- ◯ They had no other place to live.

2 **What is one way that a castle in Japan was different from a castle in England?**

- ◯ It had a moat.
- ◯ It was built as a fort.
- ◯ It was built with inner and outer walls.
- ◯ It was made of wood.

3 **Why did people build castles?**

- ◯ to create better farms
- ◯ to protect themselves
- ◯ to make fairy tales come true
- ◯ to have a quiet place to live

4 **How are castles in Japan and England alike?**

- ◯ Both had inner and outer walls and moats.
- ◯ Both had lords and ladies and warriors living in them.
- ◯ They were made of the same materials.
- ◯ They looked the same.

5 **What is probably the main difference between the use of castles today and the use of castles long ago?**

___

___

___

___

___

___

___

Name ___________________________________

Read the selection. Then answer the questions that follow.

Two Famous Athletes

Tiger Woods and Michael Jordan are two of the most famous names and faces in sports. Both men have been on magazine covers, on television, and on cereal boxes.

Michael Jordan has been called the best basketball player in the history of the game, so it's surprising to learn that when he was in high school he did not make the varsity basketball team in his sophomore year. However, he did not give up. He worked very hard to become a good player, and the next year he joined the team. As a professional, he was a leader for the Chicago Bulls.

Jordan's leadership extended off the court too. He opened the James R. Jordan Boys and Girls Club and Family Center, named after his father. The center gives the people of Chicago a safe place to relax and have fun.

Tiger Woods is one of the world's most famous golfers. He swung his first golf club when he was only eleven months old. He also won every junior golf tournament he entered. At eighteen, he was the youngest player ever to win the U.S. Amateur tournament, and he is the only golfer ever to win it three times in a row.

Like Michael Jordan, Tiger Woods wanted to use his success to help young people, so he created the Tiger Woods Foundation. The foundation provides opportunities for less fortunate children to participate in many types of worthwhile activities.

Jordan and Woods are two champions who also care about and help others.

Turn the page.

Answer the questions below.

1 **How are Michael Jordan and Tiger Woods alike?**

- ◯ Both showed special talent when they were very young.
- ◯ Both have worked hard to help other people.
- ◯ Both were the youngest ever to win major awards.
- ◯ Both were the highest scorers for their teams.

2 **What is one way that Michael Jordan and Tiger Woods are different?**

- ◯ Jordan likes sports, and Woods does not.
- ◯ Jordan played sports in high school, and Woods started in middle school.
- ◯ Jordan plays a team sport, and Woods does not.
- ◯ Jordan is well-known, and Woods is not.

3 **Michael Jordan was finally able to join his high school team because**

- ◯ his father was hired as the head coach there.
- ◯ he was the best basketball player in history.
- ◯ he worked and became a good enough player.
- ◯ he was the tallest leader of the Chicago Bulls.

4 **Which of these two athletes is your favorite? Why?**

____

____

____

____

____

____

5 **How are the organizations these two athletes started the same?**

____

____

____

____

Name ______________________________

Read the selection. Then answer the questions that follow.

Popcorn

Popcorn is the best snack. Popcorn has been a part of meals and a snack for a long time. In fact, in the early 1700s, boys and girls ate popcorn with milk and sugar for breakfast.

Popcorn is easy to grow. Corn seeds are planted in warm weather. They grow into tall plants with ears of corn. The ears are picked about ten weeks after the kernels begin to grow. When the kernels are taken off the ear, the popcorn is ready to pop.

Popcorn tastes best during a movie. It also makes a beautiful holiday decoration. Birds eat popcorn too.

The next time you are hungry or want to feed the birds, you might want to pop some corn.

Turn the page.

Answer the questions below.

1 **Today, when do most Americans eat popcorn?**

- ◯ at Thanksgiving
- ◯ at snack time
- ◯ at breakfast
- ◯ at holidays

2 **What is the *second* paragraph mostly about?**

- ◯ what popcorn looks like
- ◯ how long popcorn grows
- ◯ when to plant popcorn
- ◯ how to grow popcorn

3 **According to the selection, what kind of animal eats popcorn?**

- ◯ pigs
- ◯ dogs
- ◯ birds
- ◯ squirrels

4 **How is your breakfast the same or different from some breakfasts in the 1700s?**

Name ______________________________________

Read the selection. Then answer the questions that follow.

Prickly Pear Cactus

Looking at the prickly pear cactus with its flat pads and inch-long thorns, you might think that it is not a useful plant, but you would be mistaken. People all over the world use the beautiful prickly pear cactus for many things.

Luther Burbank, a plant scientist, began studying the prickly pear cactus plants many years ago. He learned that if cactus plants are planted close together, they can grow to form a hedge ten to twenty feet high. This type of wall can keep out many animals.

Like all cactus plants, the prickly pears do not need much water and can live in almost any kind of dirt. They can be planted in places that do not have many plants at all. Thus, they help keep the soil in place.

Juice from the pads of the prickly pear is very useful. If you have burned yourself, you can put the juice on the burn to make it feel better. Some people mix the juice with other materials and use it on buildings to make them last longer.

The fresh pads of a prickly pear cactus without thorns can be fed to pigs and sheep. People can also eat the pads. Prickly pear jelly, bread, and soups are delicious. Even the seeds can be dried and made into flour.

Even though the prickly pear cactus may not look like a treasure, many people think it is a gem.

Turn the page.

Answer the questions below.

1 **What is the second paragraph *mostly* about?**

- ○ how to take care of this cactus
- ○ why people plant this cactus
- ○ what a scientist learned about this cactus
- ○ when people should use this cactus

2 **Paragraph 4 is mostly about which part of the prickly pear cactus?**

- ○ the thorns
- ○ the juice
- ○ the seeds
- ○ the pads

3 **Prickly pear cactus is used for all these things *except***

- ○ food.
- ○ walls.
- ○ medicine.
- ○ tires.

4 **How are the prickly pear cactus and all other cactus plants alike?**

- ○ They need a special type of dirt.
- ○ They do not need much water to grow.
- ○ They were studied by Luther Burbank.
- ○ They grow ten to twenty feet high.

5 **Describe two uses of the prickly pear cactus.**

Name ______________________________

Read the selection. Then answer the questions that follow.

Frozen Rain

Have you ever heard of rain freezing in the summer? Well, frozen rain can fall out of a strong summer thunderstorm in the form of hail.

Hail begins as a thundercloud that contains "supercooled" water. "Supercooled" water does not freeze, even though its temperature is below freezing. The water needs to touch something solid in order to freeze. As it freezes around ice crystals, frozen raindrops, dust, or salt from the ocean, it is carried upward by wind currents and gathers more water. When the ball of ice is too heavy to remain in the cloud, it drops to the Earth as ice. The hail does not melt as it falls because it is not in the air long enough. A hailstorm is an exciting sight.

If you cut a hailstone in half, it would look like the inside of an onion. The rings give information about how the hailstorm was formed.

Most hail is smaller than a dime, but the largest hailstone was more than seventeen inches around (more than five inches in diameter) and weighed about one and a half pounds.

Although hailstorms usually last for only about fifteen minutes, they can cause a lot of damage. Hail can fall to Earth as fast as ninety miles per hour, and when it hits farm crops or windows, it can seriously damage them.

The next time you see little iceballs falling out of the sky, be sure to wait before you go outside.

Turn the page.

Answer the questions below.

1 **Hail freezes around all these things *except***

- ◯ air.
- ◯ dust.
- ◯ salt.
- ◯ ice crystals.

2 **How large is most hail?**

- ◯ about one and a half pounds
- ◯ smaller than a dime
- ◯ more than five inches across
- ◯ larger than a quarter

3 **What is the *second* paragraph mostly about?**

- ◯ how hail forms
- ◯ why hail does not melt
- ◯ how exciting hail is
- ◯ what is inside of hailstones

4 **Why does the author compare hail to an onion?**

____

____

____

____

____

____

5 **What is paragraph 5 mostly about?**

____

____

____

____

____

Name ______________________________________

Read the selection. Then answer the questions that follow.

"Ground Nut" Butter

Did you know that most nuts grow on trees? That's why peanuts are sometimes called "ground nuts." Peanuts belong to the same plant family as beans and peas. They actually grow underground.

Farmers dig up the peanuts using special machines. They leave the peanuts on the ground to dry for two days or more. Then they dry the peanuts with warm air.

Many of the dried raw peanuts are used to make peanut butter. This is how it is made. First the peanuts are taken out of their shells. Then the peanuts are roasted and cooled. A machine takes off the red skin. Then the pieces are ground up until the peanuts are smooth like butter. The peanut butter is then put into jars and sold.

The next time you ask for a sandwich, make it "ground nut" butter and jelly.

Turn the page.

Answer the questions below.

1 **What is the first step in making peanut butter?**

- ◯ The shell is removed.
- ◯ A machine takes off the red skin.
- ◯ The peanuts are ground up.
- ◯ The peanuts are roasted.

2 **When are peanuts ready to leave the farm?**

- ◯ while the peanuts are in the field
- ◯ after the shells are removed
- ◯ after the peanuts have been dried
- ◯ two days after digging them up

3 **When could you ask for a "ground nut" sandwich?**

- ◯ after a jar of peanut butter has been sold
- ◯ when the farmers dry peanuts with warm air
- ◯ when the peanuts have been taken out of their shells
- ◯ when the peanuts are being ground up

4 **From this selection, what can you conclude about "ground nuts" and peanuts?**

Name ________________________________

Read the selection. Then answer the questions that follow.

Build a Castle

You can build your very own castle if you have a plan and lots of sand. The next time you are on a sandy beach, just follow these simple steps.

First, imagine the kind of castle you would like to make and, if you want to, draw a diagram on a piece of paper. Then find a place to build your castle that is not too close or too far away from the water. Near your spot, dig a hole with your hands until you find sand that is very wet. This is the sand you will scoop out and use to make your castle.

Begin by making towers from the wet sand you scooped. Take some sand and shape it into a pancake, making a big pancake for the bottom and smaller pancakes as you stack them up into a tower. After you make one tower, pour a little water on it to help keep the tower from falling apart. Then build another tower and pour water on that one, and keep making towers until you have as many as you want according to your diagram.

You can connect the towers by making walls between them. To make the walls, take some wet sand and shape it into a brick. Put one brick on top of another one until your wall is as high as you want.

Finally, smooth the walls and towers with a flat tool like a small sand shovel. Then step back and admire your castle.

Once the tide comes in, you will have to build a new castle all over again the next day!

Turn the page.

Answer the questions below.

1 **In building a castle, when do you connect the towers?**

- ◯ before you make a pancake shape
- ◯ before you stack up the pancakes
- ◯ after you admire your castle
- ◯ after you make two or more towers

2 **What is the first step in making a sand castle?**

- ◯ finding some wet sand and scooping it up
- ◯ thinking about what kind of castle you want
- ◯ drawing a diagram of the castle on paper
- ◯ finding a good place to build the castle

3 **When do you use a flat tool to smooth the walls?**

- ◯ after building the walls
- ◯ before you pour a little water on the towers
- ◯ before you make the towers
- ◯ while you are digging the hole

4 **When should you pour water on the towers?**

- ◯ as soon as one tower dries
- ◯ just before the towers fall
- ◯ after you make each tower
- ◯ after you have as many towers as you want

5 **Why would you have to rebuild your sand castle the next day?**

Name ___________________________________

Read the selection. Then answer the questions that follow.

Ready to Cook

Cooking can be fun, and following some simple rules and ideas will help you.

Once you decide what you want to make, carefully read the recipe with an adult. This person can show you how to use any tools you may need and answer any of your questions.

Next, be sure you are wearing the right clothes. Wear shirts with short sleeves, and wear an apron to keep your clothes clean. If you have long hair, keep it away from the food by tying it back.

Once you are dressed for cooking, gather together all the food and tools you will need, such as pans and measuring spoons and cups.

Be sure you have potholders to handle pans that are hot. And don't forget to have paper towels or a damp cloth near you so that you can clean up right away any food that spills. Food on the floor can make you slip and fall.

Once you have everything you need to start, always wash your hands with soap and water before you touch the food.

Finally, after you are done cooking, put away all the food you did not use in your recipe, and wash and put away any dishes or pots you used.

Following these rules before and after you cook will keep you safe and help make you a good cook.

Turn the page.

Answer the questions below.

1 **What do you do before you get out the food you need for the recipe?**

- ◯ Wash your hands.
- ◯ Put on an apron.
- ◯ Wash the pots you used.
- ◯ Find some potholders.

2 **When should you wash your hands?**

- ◯ before you get the tools you will need
- ◯ before you tie your hair back
- ◯ before you begin to handle the food
- ◯ before you clean up any spills

3 **What do you do after you finish cooking?**

- ◯ Wash your hands again.
- ◯ Read the recipe carefully.
- ◯ Make sure you have potholders.
- ◯ Clean up the kitchen.

4 **What is the first thing you do after you choose your recipe and why?**

____

____

____

____

____

____

5 **What is the goal of most of these cooking rules?**

____

____

____

____

____

Name ___________________________________

Read the selection. Then answer the questions that follow.

Model T

Many people think that Henry Ford made the first car, but people were driving cars before Henry Ford made the Model T. People also used horses and wagons or rode on trains. Cars cost a lot of money.

Henry Ford made a car that almost anyone could buy. He did this by changing the way cars were made. His factory had a moving belt that carried car parts past workers as they stood in a line. Each worker did just one part of the job. Building cars this way saved money.

In 1925 a Model T cost only $260. It was not fancy, and the only color it was made in was black. People loved it. They started to trade their horses for Model Ts. Our life has never been the same.

Turn the page.

Answer the questions below.

1 **What conclusion can you draw about Henry Ford?**

- ◯ He was mostly interested in making luxury cars.
- ◯ He was more interested in helping people than in making money.
- ◯ He believed that people would buy more cars if they cost less.
- ◯ He wanted to change the way roads were built.

2 **In Henry Ford's factory, what happened after one worker did his job for one part of a car?**

- ◯ The workers then got into a long line.
- ◯ The moving belt changed directions.
- ◯ The next worker did his job on another part.
- ◯ The moving belt stopped to take a rest break.

3 **Why did so many people buy Henry Ford's cars?**

- ◯ because he was making cars before the Model T
- ◯ because the Model T was the first black car
- ◯ because he taught workers how to do part of the job
- ◯ because he built cars that they could afford

4 **What is one way life was different before people owned cars?**

Name ___________________________________

Read the selection. Then answer the questions that follow.

Bird Songs

You probably hear birds singing every day, but did you ever wonder how and why they sing?

Birds sing by using something called a syrinx. It is a tube with two sides, deep inside the bird's chest, which allows the bird to sing two notes at the same time, or to breathe through one side and sing with the other. Birds can make trilling sounds and chuckling sounds, as well as many, many more.

As you probably know, some birds can even talk. Parrots can talk because they have thick tongues, as humans do, to shape the sounds they make with the syrinx. Smaller birds, like budgies, use their syrinx in special ways to make human sounds.

Not all birds sing, but all birds make particular sounds to communicate with other birds. We call these sounds bird calls. Birds call to announce danger and may have several calls to describe different kinds of danger. They call to mark the borders of the area where they live. To guard their surroundings, birds call to tell other birds to stay away.

Male birds use their calls hoping that female birds will like them so they can begin families. The male bird's call is also intended to scare away other male birds that are looking for a female. Young birds make distress calls, which bring adult birds to their aid. Young birds also make feeding calls, which say they're very hungry and need food right now!

Now when you hear a bird singing or calling, you will know that it is sending an important message.

Turn the page.

Answer the questions below.

1 Before a bird makes a danger call, it *most likely*

- ◯ has produced a human sound.
- ◯ has gotten food for its young.
- ◯ has been scared by something.
- ◯ has warned its family already.

2 After reading this selection, what can you conclude about bird calls?

- ◯ Birds call only when they cannot sing.
- ◯ Bird calls are more beautiful than bird songs.
- ◯ Calls are the way birds talk to each other.
- ◯ Calls are made mostly to tell other birds what to do.

3 What can you conclude about the bird sounds?

- ◯ Bird calls are more varied than bird songs.
- ◯ All birds can sing.
- ◯ All birds sing, but only some birds call.
- ◯ All birds call, but only some birds sing.

4 What can you conclude about birds that make feeding calls?

- ◯ They are warning other birds to stay away.
- ◯ They are very young birds.
- ◯ They have found food for their babies.
- ◯ They are flying around looking for food.

5 What kind of danger do you think a bird call might tell about?

Name ___________________________________

Read the selection. Then answer the questions that follow.

Amazing Snakes

When most people hear the word *snake*, they think of something slimy and dangerous. In fact, snakes are not slimy and are only dangerous if you scare them or bother them. Some people even want snakes around their homes or barns because snakes eat rats, mice, and insects.

Snakes are amazing because they do not have legs, ears, or eyelids, yet they can do all the things other animals can do, such as hunt and protect themselves.

All snakes have clear scales over their eyes instead of eyelids, which is why they always look wide-awake.

Snakes use their forked tongues to smell, so when a snake is hungry, it tastes the ground or air with its tongue; then it brings the tongue to a special sense organ in its mouth that tells the snake what it has smelled. If it smells something it wants to eat, it follows the scent.

Snakes protect themselves in different ways. Some snakes hiss, and some shake the rattles on their tails as a warning, while others play dead, hoping that the ground will hide them. Some rely on looking like the ground or woods where they live.

All snakes are cold-blooded. This means that their body temperature depends on the temperature outside their bodies. This is why snakes look for shady, cool spots when it is hot out and sunny rocks to lie on when it's cold.

Some people say that snakes make the best pets because they only eat once a week and do not need to go for a walk. Don't let them fool you. It is not that easy to give a good home to the amazing snake.

Turn the page.

Answer the questions below.

1 **What conclusion can you draw about snakes based on the selection?**

- ◯ Snakes are not dangerous.
- ◯ Snakes may be dangerous if you surprise them.
- ◯ Snakes are always dangerous.
- ◯ Snakes are only dangerous if the weather is warm.

2 **Why do you think the author says that snakes are amazing?**

- ◯ because they are so different from us
- ◯ because they are able to protect themselves
- ◯ because they eat mice
- ◯ because they are not slimy

3 **What does a snake do after it smells something it wants to eat?**

- ◯ It shakes its rattles loudly to frighten it.
- ◯ It plays dead to stay hidden from it.
- ◯ It uses its tongue to follow its scent.
- ◯ It warms up its body on the sunny rocks.

4 **Why would it not do any good to yell at a snake to scare it away?**

____

____

____

____

____

____

5 **In what two ways are snakes useful to humans?**

____

____

____

____

____

Name ____________________________________

Read the selection. Then answer the questions that follow.

Friend of Nature

Some people say that Rachel Carson was a hero. Others say she was foolish. No matter what people say about her, she will always be remembered.

Rachel Carson wrote books about the world of nature in which we live. Her final book, *Silent Spring,* warned about the dangers of poisons used to kill insects. These poisons are called pesticides. She told about how they killed birds as well as insects. She told about dangers to fish and other creatures. She called for changes in the use of these poisons. Many people who produced and used the pesticides fought against Rachel's ideas for making those changes. For Rachel Carson, it was important to keep the world safe for all living things. She courageously wrote to tell people how she felt.

People will always thank this brave woman. She taught us that keeping all living things safe is every person's job.

Turn the page.

Answer the questions below.

1 What was the author's main purpose in writing this selection?

- ○ to persuade the reader to admire Rachel Carson
- ○ to give some facts about Rachel Carson's life
- ○ to warn against the use of pesticides
- ○ to describe Rachel Carson's feelings

2 Why did the author describe Rachel Carson as brave?

- ○ to show that she was very popular
- ○ to make the reader curious
- ○ to tell how everyone felt about her
- ○ to show that she was able to stand up to others

3 You can conclude from this selection that Rachel Carson

- ○ lived near the ocean.
- ○ worked for a newspaper.
- ○ cared deeply about the Earth.
- ○ taught college students.

4 Why did the author say that some people thought Rachel Carson was foolish?

Name ______________________________

Read the selection. Then answer the questions that follow.

Wolves of the Sea

The orca, or killer whale, is the biggest animal in the dolphin family. Like other dolphins, it has a blowhole on the top of its head so it can breathe air. Killer whales live and hunt together in families called pods, much the way wolves in a pack live and hunt together. This is why killer whales are sometimes called wolves of the sea.

Each pod makes its own special sound so that the whales that live in the same pod can recognize their family. The clicks and whistles killer whales make also help them communicate when they're hunting.

Killer whales are black with white patches. They can grow to be as long as twenty-eight feet and weigh twelve thousand pounds or more. They have teeth in both jaws, each tooth being about three inches long and one inch in diameter. Killer whales can swim as fast as thirty miles per hour when they are chasing their prey. They will eat almost any sea animal, including turtles, seals, other whales, and even birds.

These beautiful black-and-white whales live all over the world. People are sometimes lucky enough to see the giants when they leap out of the water. Killer whales also like to slap their tails on top of the water, but no one knows why they do these things.

Because they are so beautiful and easy to train, they are often used in movies and marine animal shows, working closely with people.

Whether you see a killer whale in a movie, in a park, or in the ocean, it will be a sight you will never forget.

Turn the page.

Answer the questions below.

1 Why did the author write this selection?

- ○ to make you want to protect killer whales
- ○ to inform you about killer whales
- ○ to describe how killer whales hunt
- ○ to warn you about a dangerous animal

2 Why did the author use the words *clicks* and *whistles* to describe the sounds the whales make?

- ○ because other whales use clicks and whistles
- ○ to show that whales sound like humans
- ○ to let you know that the author has heard whales
- ○ to help you understand how whales sound

3 Why did the author probably use the term *killer whales* more often than *orcas?*

- ○ *Killer whales* is the more scientific term.
- ○ *Killer whales* sounds more exciting than *orcas.*
- ○ The term *killer whales* is shorter than the term *orcas.*
- ○ There are more *killer whales* than there are *orcas.*

4 What is the author's purpose for including the third paragraph?

- ○ to express feelings about the way orcas hunt their prey
- ○ to inform you about how orcas talk to each other
- ○ to help you enjoy orcas if you see them
- ○ to inform you about the size and speed of the orca

5 The selection states that seeing a killer whale is something you will never forget. What do you think is the *most likely* reason that this might be true?

Name ___________________________________

Read the selection. Then answer the questions that follow.

The White House

Next to the flag, the White House is my favorite symbol of our government.

When George Washington was President in 1790, he chose the site for this special home for Presidents and oversaw its construction beginning in 1792. The White House was finished eight years later, but he never lived in it because there was a new President. John Adams moved into the house in 1800, and since then every President has lived there.

The White House has six floors (two of them basements), 132 rooms, thirty-two bathrooms, three elevators, and seven staircases. Of the six floors, two are for the President, his family, and important guests, so visitors cannot go there. But visitors can see the two public floors, and about six thousand people visit them every day.

The White House does not look the same today as it did when it was first built. Wings and floors were added as Presidents needed more room for office space. Also, because the White House is the President's private home, every President can change the way the rooms look to make his home special for him. But the outside walls of the White House are the same as when it was first built. The stone walls are painted white, and it takes 570 gallons of paint to cover them. The President's house was first officially named the White House in 1901, when Theodore Roosevelt lived there.

You should try to visit the White House, if not in person, then in books. You'll be glad you did.

Turn the page.

Answer the questions below.

1 Why did the author write this selection?

- ◯ to tell the reader how Presidents live
- ◯ to express patriotic feelings about the White House
- ◯ to explain how the White House was built
- ◯ to make the reader want to visit the White House

2 Why did the author tell you the number of rooms and floors in the White House?

- ◯ to help you understand how big it is
- ◯ to show you how hard it is to get around inside
- ◯ to let you know that not all the rooms are open to visitors
- ◯ to tell you about the history of the building

3 You can conclude from this selection that

- ◯ leaders of other countries might stay at the White House.
- ◯ George Washington lived at the White House.
- ◯ future presidents will not live at the White House.
- ◯ the White House looks the same as when it was built.

4 Why did the author tell you some of the history of the White House?

____

____

____

____

____

____

5 Why did the author call the White House a symbol of our government?

____

____

____

____

____

Name ____

Read the selection. Then answer the questions that follow.

An Orange a Day

For years people have been saying that we should eat fruits and vegetables every day. Why are fruits and vegetables so important?

First of all, fruits and vegetables have vitamin C. Vitamin C is important to help your body fight germs so that you stay healthy. Vitamin C helps heal cuts on your body. It also keeps your gums healthy. Our bodies do not make vitamin C, so we have to get it by eating fruits, such as oranges, and vegetables, such as green and red peppers. To get the most vitamin C from fruits and vegetables, you should eat them soon after you bring them home. Letting fruits get too old destroys the vitamins in them.

They say an apple a day keeps the doctor away. Maybe you should eat an orange a day too.

Turn the page.

Answer the questions below.

1 **Which of the following sentences from the selection is a statement of opinion?**

- ○ First of all, fruits and vegetables have vitamin C.
- ○ Maybe you should eat an orange a day too.
- ○ Vitamin C helps heal cuts on your body.
- ○ It also keeps your gums healthy.

2 **Why did the author *most likely* write this selection?**

- ○ to compare and contrast fruits and vegetables
- ○ to inform you about different vitamins
- ○ to explain what you should do to get rid of a cold
- ○ to persuade you to eat more fruits and vegetables

3 **Which of the following *best* describes this selection?**

- ○ It contains all statements of opinion.
- ○ It contains many false statements.
- ○ It contains mostly statements of fact.
- ○ It contains opinions, but no supporting facts.

4 **Write a statement of fact from the selection. Explain why this is a statement of fact.**

Name ______________________________________

Read the selection. Then answer the questions that follow.

"Strong Mind, Strong Body"

Exercising is the best way to keep your body strong and your mind sharp. When you run around on the playground or play tag with your friends, not only are you having fun, but you are also improving your body and mind.

Exercise helps your heart stay strong by making it beat faster, and a strong heart will do a better job of getting oxygen to all parts of your body. To make your heart beat faster, try swimming or jumping rope or doing almost anything that works up a sweat. You do not need to buy anything special.

Exercise builds strong muscles and bones. To make your muscles stronger you have to do powerful things, like swinging across the monkey bars at school or lifting heavy things. These exercises will also help build strong bones.

Exercise helps you bend and stretch your body comfortably, which is important when you want to move your arms and legs without hurting them. If you cannot touch your toes, you need to exercise. Dancing and tumbling are two of the best ways to help your body stretch more easily.

Exercise is a great way to help you feel good about yourself. When you run and jump, you feel strong and proud of yourself. Your body also releases special chemicals called endorphins that actually make you feel happy.

Exercise helps your brain too. Some people think that exercising helps the blood (and oxygen) flow to your brain so you can think better and pay attention longer.

No matter what kind of exercise you do, you should get moving every day to be healthy and happy.

Turn the page.

Answer the questions below.

1 **Why did the author write this selection?**

- ○ to state an opinion about stretching
- ○ to compare different exercises
- ○ to explain all about the heart
- ○ to persuade you to exercise

2 **Which of these sentences from the selection is a statement of opinion?**

- ○ Exercise helps your heart stay strong.
- ○ Exercise builds strong muscles and bones.
- ○ You should get moving every day.
- ○ You do not need to buy anything special.

3 **Which of these is a statement of fact?**

- ○ Exercising is the best way to keep your body strong and your mind sharp.
- ○ Exercise is a great way to help you feel good about yourself.
- ○ Dancing and tumbling are two of the best ways to help you stretch.
- ○ A strong heart will do a better job of getting oxygen to all parts of your body.

4 **The author writes, "When you can run and jump, you feel strong and proud of yourself." Which of these *best* describes this statement?**

- ○ It is a statement of opinion.
- ○ It is a statement of fact.
- ○ It is both a statement of fact and opinion.
- ○ It is a false statement.

5 **How could you check about the facts contained in this selection?**

___

___

___

___

___

___

___

Name ______________________________

Read the selection. Then answer the questions that follow.

Sweet Dreams

All animals sleep, some standing up and others reclining, and, of course, humans need sleep too. No one really knows how our brains and bodies are occupied when we sleep. Nevertheless, we do understand that it is absolutely necessary that we get adequate sleep.

It looks as if nothing is happening when we are sleeping, but our bodies and brains are actually quite active. Our bodies are constructing the new cells that we need to grow and repairing any cell damage that occurred during the day. Sleep also helps our immune system destroy germs that can make us ill. Without sleep, children do not grow, and we all may get sick more frequently. During sleep, our brains organize information and store memories.

Most individuals love to sleep. People who do not get enough sleep make errors, forget things, get upset easily, and even lose their ability to tell reality from fantasy.

Everyone needs sleep, but the amount of sleep we require changes as we age. A newborn baby sleeps from sixteen to twenty hours a day, but as people grow older, they need less sleep. The average ten-year-old sleeps ten hours a day, while most adults spend about eight hours snoozing. Some older people only spend about five hours asleep. That is not very much.

We look and feel better after a good night's sleep, and our bodies and brains are ready for a new day. So, make sure you get enough sleep! Going to bed on time is considerably more important than staying up late to watch television.

Turn the page.

Answer the questions below.

1 **Which of these is a statement of fact?**

- ◯ Going to bed on time is more important than watching television.
- ◯ So, make sure you get enough sleep!
- ◯ During sleep, our brains organize information and store memories.
- ◯ Most people love to sleep.

2 **Which of these is a statement of opinion?**

- ◯ A newborn baby sleeps from sixteen to twenty hours a day.
- ◯ All animals sleep, some standing up and others reclining.
- ◯ As people grow older, they need less sleep.
- ◯ Five hours of sleep is not very much.

3 **What would be the *best* source of information about sleep?**

- ◯ an encyclopedia article about sleep
- ◯ a television commercial for a mattress
- ◯ a book about helping babies sleep
- ◯ an Internet article about the brain

4 **Why do you think the author wrote this selection?**

5 **Write another statement of fact from the selection. Explain how you know it is a statement of fact.**

Name ____

Read the selection. Then answer the questions that follow.

The Mouse and the Lion

Mouse wanted to be just like his friend Lion. After Mouse helped Lion escape from a hunter's net, Lion roared so loudly that the trees shook.

Mouse was amazed. He had a small voice, but he wanted to roar like Lion.

"If I practice," thought Mouse, "I'll be able to roar."

So he started practicing. Mouse opened his mouth wide, took a deep breath, and squeaked. Disappointed, Mouse tried again, but he could not roar, no matter how many times he tried.

"Lion is tall," thought Mouse. "I'll climb a small tree so I can be as tall as Lion. Then I will roar."

Mouse climbed a holly bush, and now he was as tall as Lion, who was nearby watching Mouse.

Mouse opened his mouth wide, took a deep breath, and squeaked. He tried again, but he could not roar.

"Mouse, you should do the special thing that only a mouse can do," said Lion.

Mouse hurried home to practice squeaking.

Turn the page.

Answer the questions below.

1 **What did Mouse learn in this story?**

- ◯ It is better to do what you know how to do than to try something new.
- ◯ It is better to be a mouse than a lion.
- ◯ It is better to concentrate on your strengths than on your weaknesses.
- ◯ Mouse could be as brave as a lion even if he could not roar.

2 **Why did Mouse want to roar?**

- ◯ because he liked the way Lion sounded
- ◯ because he wanted to be friends with Lion
- ◯ because he wanted to frighten hunters away
- ◯ because he had a small voice that squeaked

3 **Why couldn't Mouse learn to roar?**

- ◯ because only tall animals can roar
- ◯ because he stopped practicing
- ◯ because Mouse was not special
- ◯ because he was not a lion

4 **Why did Mouse climb a holly tree?**

Name ____________________________________

Read the selection. Then answer the questions that follow.

Spike's Blue Ribbon

Spike wanted a blue ribbon. All of his friends had at least one ribbon, and they laughed at Spike and told him he would never win a ribbon because his legs were too short and one of his ears would not stand up straight.

Spike was a busy dog, so he did not think about ribbons often. He had to take care of Emma, and that took up all of his time and energy. Every day he had to take Emma for a walk and then let her throw a ball so he could catch it and give it back to her. Emma liked this game, so Spike and Emma did this until Emma got tired. After supper Spike had to sit next to Emma while she did her homework, and later he had to watch Emma until she fell asleep, so by the time he went to bed, Spike was tired.

One night as Spike was watching Emma sleep, he smelled something he had never smelled before, and it made him anxious. Spike jumped off Emma's bed and began to sniff around, and pretty soon he felt hot and his eyes started to hurt. *Fire,* thought Spike, and he started barking to tell Emma to get out, but Emma's mom and dad heard Spike first. They got Emma and ran outside, with Spike running right behind them. When Spike heard the fire truck, he barked to let them know help was coming.

Later everyone said that Spike was a hero, and Emma told Spike he was the best dog in the world. Finally Spike knew how it felt to win a blue ribbon.

Turn the page.

Answer the questions below.

1 **Why did Spike bark to tell Emma to get out?**
- ◯ because he wanted to win a blue ribbon
- ◯ because he heard a truck coming to the house
- ◯ because he realized there was a fire in the house
- ◯ because Emma would not wake up

2 **What did Spike learn in this story?**
- ◯ You do not need a blue ribbon to be a winner.
- ◯ Emma's mom and dad could smell fire.
- ◯ Barking is a good way to talk to people.
- ◯ It is more important to play games than to win ribbons.

3 **Why did Emma tell Spike he was the best dog in the world?**
- ◯ because he heard the fire truck
- ◯ because he saved the family
- ◯ because he finally won a ribbon
- ◯ because he slept on her bed

4 **Why did the other dogs laugh at Spike?**
- ◯ because he spent so much time with Emma
- ◯ because he never tried to win a ribbon
- ◯ because he did not want to play with them
- ◯ because he was not a very good-looking dog

5 **Why did Spike spend so much time with Emma?**

____

____

____

____

____

____

____

Name ____

Read the selection. Then answer the questions that follow.

Alfonso's Pet

Alfonso wanted a budgie from Australia. He learned about budgies when his class was studying animals that lived in other countries. Alfonso thought budgies were beautiful birds. Also, because they were small parrots, he hoped he could teach his budgie to talk.

When Alfonso asked his mom if he could get a budgie, she told him that they cost too much money. Alfonso reminded his mom that he had saved his allowance. The next time Alfonso asked his mom for a budgie, she reminded him that taking care of a pet was hard work and had to be done every day. Alfonso promised his mom that he would take care of the bird every day after school. Alfonso's mom told him that a budgie needed a special cage, but Alfonso told his mom that he already had a cage that a friend had given him. Alfonso's mom reminded him that budgies needed special food, but Alfonso showed his mom seeds he had already bought, and even told his mom that he would call his budgie Petey.

Alfonso's mom finally agreed. When Alfonso got Petey home, he put the bird into its cage, fed it, and said "Hello" over and over again, hoping Petey would learn to say it too. Every day Alfonso fed Petey, cleaned his cage, and said, "Hello." Petey ate the food, played with his toys, but never said a word. Alfonso's mom did not have to remind him to take care of Petey. Alfonso played with Petey every day and taught him to do tricks, and Petey helped Alfonso do his homework by sitting on Alfonso's desk. Soon Alfonso forgot that Petey did not talk. He liked Petey just as he was, quiet and beautiful.

Turn the page.

Answer the questions below.

1 **Why didn't Alfonso's mom want him to get a budgie?**

- ◯ She did not like budgies.
- ◯ She did not like birds.
- ◯ She thought Alfonso did not have time for a pet.
- ◯ She thought Alfonso would not take care of it.

2 **Why do you think Petey sat on Alfonso's desk when Alfonso did his homework?**

- ◯ Alfonso's desk was near Petey's cage.
- ◯ Petey liked being near Alfonso.
- ◯ Petey wanted Alfonso to do his homework.
- ◯ Alfonso fed Petey at his desk.

3 **What did Alfonso learn in this story?**

- ◯ He could be happy even if things didn't go the way he hoped.
- ◯ Having a pet was not as much fun as he thought it would be.
- ◯ It was easy to teach budgies to talk.
- ◯ Birds do not make good pets.

4 **Why did Alfonso stop trying to teach Petey to talk?**

____

____

____

____

____

____

5 **Why do you think Alfonso got a cage and seeds before he got Petey?**

____

____

____

____

____

Name ___________________________________

Read the selection. Then answer the questions that follow.

Chew on This!

Teeth are some of the best tools to have. Most animals have them, though some do not. Teeth are shaped for different uses.

Animals that eat meat have sharp front teeth to bite, hold, and kill their food. They use their teeth to tear their food, not to chew it that much.

Plant eaters have flat back teeth to chew their food well before swallowing it.

Animals that eat both meat and plants, such as people do, have both sharp and flat teeth.

Animals without any teeth have to use other mouth parts, such as their tongues or beaks, to catch and eat their food.

What is more, teeth are not just used for eating. Some animals use their teeth for digging, fighting, cutting down trees, and even moving around.

ANIMAL TEETH		
Animal	**Teeth**	**Uses**
Cow		eating plants
Frog	none	uses tongue for eating bugs
People		eating meat and plants, tearing things
Tiger	sharp	eating meat, fighting
Walrus	sharp	eating meat, digging, fighting, getting on the ice

Turn the page.

Answer the questions below.

1 **Which of these is a statement of opinion?**

- ◯ Teeth are shaped for different uses.
- ◯ Most animals have them, though some do not.
- ◯ Teeth are some of the best tools to have.
- ◯ What is more, teeth are not just used for eating.

2 **On the chart, what kind of teeth should you put in for "People"?**

- ◯ sharp
- ◯ flat
- ◯ sharp and flat
- ◯ none

3 **Based on the chart, which animal uses teeth for eating plants only?**

- ◯ cow
- ◯ frog
- ◯ tiger
- ◯ walrus

4 **What kind of teeth should you put in the chart for "Cow"? Explain why.**

Name ______________________________

Read the selection. Then answer the questions that follow.

Morse Code

What if someone said he or she would send you a message, but all you heard was four short taps, a pause, then two short taps? Would you understand the message? If you knew Morse code, you would have heard the letters *HI*.

Samuel Morse invented the Morse code about 175 years ago as part of his system for sending messages over wires. His code used a combination of short taps, or dots, and long taps, or dashes, to stand for each letter of the alphabet. By combining dots and dashes, people could send messages across the country much faster than they could by Pony Express or carrier pigeon.

The most famous three letters in Morse code are probably dot-dot-dot-dash-dash-dash-dot-dot-dot, which stands for SOS. This is a signal sent by someone who needed help. SOS saved thousands of lives at sea. Ships at sea sent the code over a wireless radio or by switching a light on or off. If the light was on for a short time, it meant a dot, and if it lasted a little longer, it was a dash.

Today, with new and better ways to stay in touch on both sea and land, Morse code is no longer used, but SOS still means a cry for help.

DOTS AND DASHES					
Letter	Morse Code	Letter	Morse Code	Letter	Morse Code
A	•–	D	–••	G	––•
B	–•••	E	•	H	••••
C	–•–•	F	••–•	I	••

Turn the page.

Answer the questions below.

1 **How does the chart help the reader understand the selection?**

- ◯ It explains a message written in Morse code.
- ◯ It shows what Morse code looks like written down.
- ◯ It explains how Morse code changed over the years.
- ◯ It shows what a Morse code machine looks like.

2 **What is another good title for the chart?**

- ◯ "Samuel Morse's Life"
- ◯ "Morse Code, a Cry for Help"
- ◯ "Sending Messages with Morse Code"
- ◯ "Sample of the Morse Alphabet"

3 **Which of these is the Morse code for the letter *F*?**

- ◯ –••
- ◯ ••–•
- ◯ ––•
- ◯ –•–•

4 **How would you send the word *HE* in Morse code?**

- ◯ •••• [pause] •
- ◯ •••• [pause] ••
- ◯ •••• [pause] •–
- ◯ ––• [pause] •

5 **What would be a good way to check the facts in this selection?**

Name ______________________________

Read the selection. Then answer the questions that follow it.

Money

Money is a part of life. When you go to the store to buy a pencil, you give someone money, and you get your pencil. Money is part of what is called an exchange system.

People need an exchange system, but they do not always use money. In the system of barter, items themselves are exchanged. For example, you might trade a dozen eggs for a dozen pencils or a cow for a rug. Of course, in bartering, it is difficult to know if the trade is fair, and trading like this can be a problem.

When people began traveling long distances to trade, they wanted something that was easy to carry and hard to damage. They began to use metals such as copper, silver, and gold because they thought the metals were valuable. When a piece of metal was stamped with an image or words, it became flat and round, much like the coins we use today.

Some people used square pieces of brightly colored leather as money. We think this was the first kind of paper money.

Money continues to change as people's demands change. With the use of computers to buy and sell things, we can now exchange money over wires.

No matter how much the shape of money changes, an exchange system will always be a part of life.

The History of Exchange

Around the World: Barter cattle, grain, etc.	Turkey: First silver bars	Turkey: First true coins	Italy: First Roman coins	China: First leather money	China: First paper money	Europe: First entirely electronic money
9,000 BC	c. 2250 BC	c. 640 BC	300 BC	118 BC	AD 806	AD 1999

Turn the page.

Answer the questions below.

1 **What is another good title for the timeline?**

- ◯ "The History of Money in China"
- ◯ "Leather and Paper Money"
- ◯ "Money Through Time"
- ◯ "Your Time Is Money"

2 **Based on the timeline, where were coins first used?**

- ◯ China
- ◯ Europe
- ◯ Italy
- ◯ Turkey

3 **According to the timeline, people in China were the first to use**

- ◯ paper money.
- ◯ gold coins.
- ◯ cattle for bartering.
- ◯ silver bars.

4 **How does the timeline help the reader better understand the selection?**

____

____

____

____

____

____

5 **Write one statement of fact about money.**

____

____

____

____

____

Name ____________________________________

Read the selection. Then answer the questions that follow.

The Lunch Room

Tyrone watched his friend Jeff push the boy who was in front of him in the lunch line. The small boy was trying hard not to cry. Tyrone wanted to help the boy, but Jeff was popular, and Tyrone did not want Jeff to be mad at him.

The next day at lunch Tyrone watched as Jeff pushed the boy's lunch tray off the table, spilling his cake and milk. Tyrone did not know what to do. If he helped the boy, Jeff would be mad at him. If he did not help the boy, he would be mad at himself.

Tyrone talked to his mom and dad about Jeff.

"Sometimes it's not easy to do the right thing," Tyrone's mom said.

The next day when Jeff began to make fun of the boy, Tyrone took a deep breath and told Jeff to stop. When the boy smiled at him, Tyrone knew he had done the right thing. It felt good.

Turn the page.

Answer the questions below.

1 **What did Tyrone learn in this story?**

- ○ His friend Jeff was doing good things after all.
- ○ His mom and dad gave him good advice.
- ○ Helping someone is the right thing to do.
- ○ You should think carefully before you do anything.

2 **Which of these was not important to the plot of the story?**

- ○ Tyrone watched his friend Jeff push a boy.
- ○ The boy had cake and milk on his lunch tray.
- ○ Tyrone did not want Jeff to be mad at him.
- ○ Tyrone talked to his mom and dad about Jeff.

3 **Why did Tyrone talk to his parents?**

- ○ because they always told him what to do
- ○ because he did not want Jeff to be mad
- ○ because Jeff was going to make fun of him
- ○ because he was confused about what to do

4 **Why didn't Tyrone help the boy at first?**

Name ___________________________________

Read the selection. Then answer the questions that follow.

Tanya's New Friend

Mr. Patel was born in India and had come to this country only six months ago with his wife and two sons. They all learned English quickly, and, although they thought about India sometimes, they were happy to be here.

One day Mr. Patel and his family came to Tanya's house for dinner. Ram Patel was Tanya's age, so Tanya's dad asked her to welcome Ram to their home. Tanya told him that she was sorry all her video games were old. She asked him if he would like to play some other games. While Tanya got out some board games, Ram looked around Tanya's room and thought that his whole village did not have as many books, toys, or clothes as this one person had.

At dinner Tanya complained that they were having chicken again. Mr. Patel told Tanya's dad that in India sometimes all they had to eat was rice, but now they had fresh vegetables every day. He said that many new friends had helped them get used furniture and clothes for his home and family. But mostly he was thankful that Ram had books and could go to school.

Tanya had never seen a person so happy about vegetables. She thought about her warm bed, her toys, and all her clothes. Her face got red when she thought how she had complained about her toys and the food.

"Dad, since you made this great meal, I'll clean up the kitchen," Tanya said as she got up to clear the table.

Turn the page.

Answer the questions below.

1 **What did Tanya learn in this story?**

- ○ She had a new friend.
- ○ Her dad was a good cook.
- ○ She was luckier than she thought.
- ○ Her video games were not so old after all.

2 **Which of these was most important to the plot of this story?**

- ○ Ram Patel came over for dinner.
- ○ They were having chicken for dinner.
- ○ Tanya got out some board games.
- ○ The Patels had two sons.

3 **Why did Tanya offer to clean up the kitchen at the end?**

- ○ She liked washing and drying the dishes.
- ○ Her father had asked her to help him.
- ○ She was happy that dinner was over.
- ○ She was ashamed of the way she had acted.

4 **Why did Tanya apologize for her video games?**

- ○ She wanted Ram to play a board game.
- ○ She thought everyone else had newer ones.
- ○ She wanted Ram to tell her about his life in India.
- ○ She did not know what games Ram had.

5 **Why did Mr. Patel tell about their life in India?**

Name ___________________________________

Read the selection. Then answer the questions that follow.

Celebrating Earth Day

Marguerite's class was studying ways of saving Earth's resources. One way was to save trees by using paper over again instead of throwing it away. A boy in Marguerite's class said that his sister made puppets out of small paper bags, and a girl said that they used comics to wrap gifts instead of buying wrapping paper. Marguerite's teacher told the class that for homework they should think of an idea for how to use paper over again.

When Marguerite got home she told her mom about her own idea. "I will make cards for birthdays and holidays using old magazines, paper bags, and the envelopes that letters came in," she said.

Marguerite gathered some paper bags her mom had saved, some old magazines and white envelopes from the recycling bin, glue, scissors, a ruler, and colored markers. Marguerite's mom gave her some pieces of ribbon and old wrapping paper.

Marguerite looked for pictures of beaches because she loved the ocean. Next, she cut the paper bags into different-sized pieces and then folded them in half. She glued a picture of a beach on one piece of brown paper, and then cut out some cloud shapes from the white paper and glued them on. Then she glued the ribbon around the picture. The front of the card looked great, and it was all made with things that would have been thrown away.

Marguerite was eager to show her card to her teacher and her friends. She decided that she would make more cards, but her first card would be to celebrate Earth Day.

Turn the page.

Answer the questions below.

1 **What did Marguerite learn in this story?**

- ○ It is easier to buy cards than to make them.
- ○ She wants to show her card to her teacher.
- ○ Saving the Earth's resources can be fun.
- ○ She does not have to wrap presents.

2 **Which of these was important to the plot of this story?**

- ○ Marguerite's teacher assigned homework.
- ○ Marguerite used a ruler and some glue to make her cards.
- ○ One student used comics to wrap gifts.
- ○ Marguerite glued ribbon around the pictures.

3 **What happened after Marguerite told her mom her idea?**

- ○ Her mom told her it was a good idea.
- ○ Marguerite hurried home from school.
- ○ Marguerite found ribbon and old wrapping paper.
- ○ Her mom helped her find things to use for the cards.

4 **Why did Marguerite want her first card to celebrate Earth Day?**

____

____

____

____

____

5 **Is it important to the plot that Marguerite used a picture of a beach on her card? Explain your answer.**

____

____

____

____

____

Name ____________________________________

Read the selection. Then answer the questions that follow.

Visit to Mexico

July 29

Dear Kailey,

Hi! I'm having so much fun here in Mexico with Grandma. Today we went to the museum where they had many huge stone sculptures.

Then we went outside to find something to eat. This was the best part of the day! We had tamales. They were delicious!

Tamales are like stuffed corn pancakes. People eat them here on the street and at home. They can be filled with almost anything. The one I ate had fish inside. Yum!

Tomorrow Grandma is taking me to the outdoor market to buy a Mexican dress. Maybe we will eat tamales again! I hope so. I could eat tamales every day.

Some day maybe Grandma can make us some tamales. I miss you!

Love,

Yoli

Turn the page.

Answer the questions below.

1 **Which of these is *most important* to the plot of this story?**

- ◯ Yoli ate a tamale.
- ◯ Yoli and Grandma went outside.
- ◯ Yoli missed Kailey.
- ◯ Yoli and Grandma went to the museum.

2 **What can you say about Yoli in general?**

- ◯ She will go to the market.
- ◯ She was having a good time.
- ◯ She ate a fish tamale.
- ◯ She saw stone sculptures.

3 **What can you say about all tamales?**

- ◯ They have fish stuffed inside them.
- ◯ They can have almost any filling.
- ◯ They are eaten outdoors on the street.
- ◯ Grandma makes the very best ones.

4 **What is another general statement that can be made about Yoli?**

Name ________________________________

Read the selection. Then answer the questions that follow.

Write a Letter!

Barry raced into his grandfather's room, shouting, "Grandpa, I just heard the town is going to knock down the skate park! It's not fair!"

"Hmm," murmured Grandpa. "Maybe you should do something about it."

"What can I do?" asked Barry.

"I'll tell you a story that'll give you your answer."

"Okay," said Barry.

"When I was a boy, a little younger than you, I had a favorite book that was called *The Little Red Lighthouse and the Great Gray Bridge,* written by Hildegard H. Swift in 1942. In the book, the little red lighthouse was afraid it would be torn down when the great gray bridge with a big light on top was constructed nearby. Lighthouses shine a light to help ships pass safely. The little red lighthouse didn't think it would be useful anymore since the big bridge had a light. When I found out it was a real, historic lighthouse, on the Hudson River, that New York City was planning to tear down, my mother helped me compose a letter to the mayor about my feelings. I was not the only one; many letters streamed into the mayor's office, and finally, the city decided to save the lighthouse because so many people cared about it."

"So, you are saying I should write a letter to the mayor?" asked Barry.

"It can't hurt," said Grandpa. "Maybe one day we could visit that little red lighthouse," Grandpa chuckled. "It's still standing."

"Cool!" said Barry. "But we'll go after I write my letter."

Turn the page.

Answer the questions below.

1 **Which of the following is a general statement?**

- ○ The little red lighthouse was afraid it would be torn down.
- ○ Lighthouses shine a light to help ships pass safely.
- ○ Barry raced into his grandfather's room, shouting.
- ○ Many letters quickly streamed into the city mayor's office.

2 **Which sentence states something about Grandpa in general?**

- ○ He wrote a letter about the red lighthouse.
- ○ He told Barry a story about a gray bridge.
- ○ He wants Barry to write some more letters.
- ○ He can have strong feelings about things.

3 **What can you say about all letters written to a mayor?**

- ○ People write them to save all the historical places.
- ○ Adults write them because they like ships and bridges.
- ○ Everyone writes them for very good reasons.
- ○ People write them because they care about something.

4 **Which of these is a general statement about the little red lighthouse?**

- ○ It is important to many people.
- ○ It was torn down years ago.
- ○ It is smaller than the gray bridge.
- ○ It was in Grandpa's favorite book.

5 **What do you think is the big idea in this story?**

Name ______________________________

Read the selection. Then answer the questions that follow.

The Math Book

After school Donna enjoyed a game of kickball with her friends; then she headed back where she had left her stuff alongside the steps. But where was her math book? Donna recalled she had deposited the book on a step nearby her backpack.

She unzipped the backpack and dug around inside. The book wasn't there. She started removing everything from the pack, but she still couldn't locate the book. Cramming all of her other possessions back in the pack, slinging it over her shoulder, and dashing back to where the other kids were still gathering their belongings, she called, "Hey, guys! Has anybody seen my math book? I left it over there with my backpack."

"I don't know," answered Toni. "What's it look like?"

"It's the new one Ms. Samms distributed last Thursday. You know, with all those colors like a swirl of oil. My mom will really be upset if I lose another schoolbook!"

"Well, I didn't notice it," Toni said, and glanced around at their other friends, who were shaking their heads negatively. "Maybe somebody found it and turned it in."

"Yeah, I'll go check," returned Donna. She hitched up her backpack and scurried up the steps to the school. As Donna entered the office, Mr. Ivory looked up from some correspondence. "Hello, Donna, did you lose something?" he inquired.

"My math book," she replied.

He held up a book with a colorful cover. "Somebody brought this in. It's fortunate that your instructor had you write your name inside. You students really need to learn to take better care of your things. It was lying on the ground outdoors."

"Oh, I will, I certainly will," Donna breathed gratefully. "Thank you."

Turn the page.

Answer the questions below.

1 **Which is a general statement you can make about this story?**

- ○ It tells all about a girl named Toni.
- ○ It describes how students play kickball.
- ○ It shows events that could really happen.
- ○ It proves that math is a difficult subject.

2 **What can you say about Donna in general?**

- ○ She has a lot of athletic friends.
- ○ She always writes her own name in her book.
- ○ She loses her new math book after school one day.
- ○ She worries about how her mother will react.

3 **What general statement can you make about the author of this story?**

- ○ She always writes books about students who lose things.
- ○ She is interested in stories about students.
- ○ She is disappointed when people are careless.
- ○ She writes stories all about playing kickball.

4 **What lesson did Donna learn in this story?**

____

____

____

____

____

____

5 **What is a general statement you can make about writing names in books?**

____

____

____

____

____